Library of
Davidson College

Astronomers at the Royal Observatory, Cape

Astronomers at the Royal Observatory Cape of Good Hope

A history with emphasis on the nineteenth century

by Brian Warner

1979
Published for the University of Cape Town by
A.A.BALKEMA Cape Town and Rotterdam

In memory of A.D.T.

522.1
W279a

Copyright (c) Brian Warner 1979
ISBN 0 86961 109 7   81 - 3582
Printed and bound by Printpak (Cape) Ltd, Cape Town

Contents

	Foreword	xi
1	FEARON FALLOWS / 1820-1831	1
2	THOMAS HENDERSON / 1831-1833	31
3	THOMAS MACLEAR / 1833-1870	37
4	EDWARD JAMES STONE / 1870-1879	73
5	DAVID GILL / 1879-1907	80
6	THE TWENTIETH CENTURY S.S.Hough (1907-23), H.Spencer-Jones (1923-33), J.Jackson (1933-50), R.H.Stoy (1950-68)	109
	Further reading	127
	Appendix : Principal staff	128
	Index	130

ILLUSTRATIONS / CREDITS / SOURCES

Sketch by C.P. Smyth. Original in Durban City Library   Frontispiece

Map of the Royal Observatory, Cape   viii/ix

1. Silhouette of Fearon Fallows. From the original in the South African Library   3

2. Impression of the proposed observatory, by the architect John Rennie. Reproduced by permission of the Public Records Office   4/5

3. Garden Rozenhof by Rev John Campbell. From Campbell's sketchbook in the South African Library   9

4. Redesigned appearance of the Observatory. Reproduced by permission of the Public Records Office   12/13

5. Ground Plan of the main building. From Volume XIX of the Memoirs of the Royal Astronomical Society   17

6. Troughton's Mural Circle at Greenwich:- a copy of which was sent to the Cape. From Pond's Astronomical Observations, Vol. I, 1826   24

7. The Royal Observatory, c. 1830, by an unknown artist. Original in the Library of Parliament   26

8. The Royal Observatory, c. 1830, by an unknown artist. Original in the Library of Parliament   26

9. Thomas Henderson. Reconstruction by Angus McBride from rough sketches by C.P. Smyth   33

10. View of the Observatory from the Flats, May 1833, by Charles D'Oyly. Original in the Cape Archives   35

11. Thomas Maclear, from The Graphic, 27 August, 1892   38

12. Cluster of huts in the grounds of the Royal Observatory; by Thomas Bowler. Original in possession of the South African Astronomical Observatory   42/3

13. Bowler pencil sketch, c. 1834. Original at the South African Astronomical Observatory   42/3

14. Bowler pencil sketch, c. 1834. Original at the South African Astronomical Observatory   42/3

15 Map of the Cape Peninsula, by Sir John Herschel. Original in the South African Library 45

16 Camera Lucida drawing by Sir John Herschel, January 1837. Original in the South African Library 47

17 Self-portrait of Charles Piazzi Smyth. Original in Gunther MS 10, Museum for the History of Science, Oxford 48

18 Apparatus employed in the Measurement of the Base Line, by C.P. Smyth. Original at the Royal Greenwich Observatory 50/51

19 Modus Operandi, by C.P.Smyth. Original at the Royal Greenwich Observatory 52/53

20 Measurement of the Parade Baseline, by C.P.Smyth. Original in the Cape Archives 54/55

21 Lithograph by C.F.Angas. From "The Colonies and India, 1877" 58/59

22 Sketch from scrapbook of Charles Midgley. Original in the South African Library 61

23 Thomas Bowler watercolour of 1854. Original in the Africana Museum 64/65

24 The Royal Observatory, by an unknown artist. Original in the Africana Museum 66

25 Map of the Royal Observatory, 1863. Redrawn from originals in the Archives of the Royal Greenwich Observatory 67

26 The Transit Circle. From the Illustrated London News 21 March 1857 68

27 Thomas Maclear's membership form for the South African Literary and Scientific Association. Original at the Royal Greenwich Observatory 69

28 Sir David Gill. Reproduced by permission of the Royal Astronomical Society 81

29 Gill's first astronomical camera. From the Cape Photographic Durchmusterung, Vol. I 91

30 Scenes at the Royal Observatory. From The Graphic, 27 August 1892 94/95

31 The McClean Dome. By Charles Peers, reproduced by permission of Galvin and Sales 99

32 Sketches at the Observatory, 1908. From the Cape Times, 19 September 1908 110/111

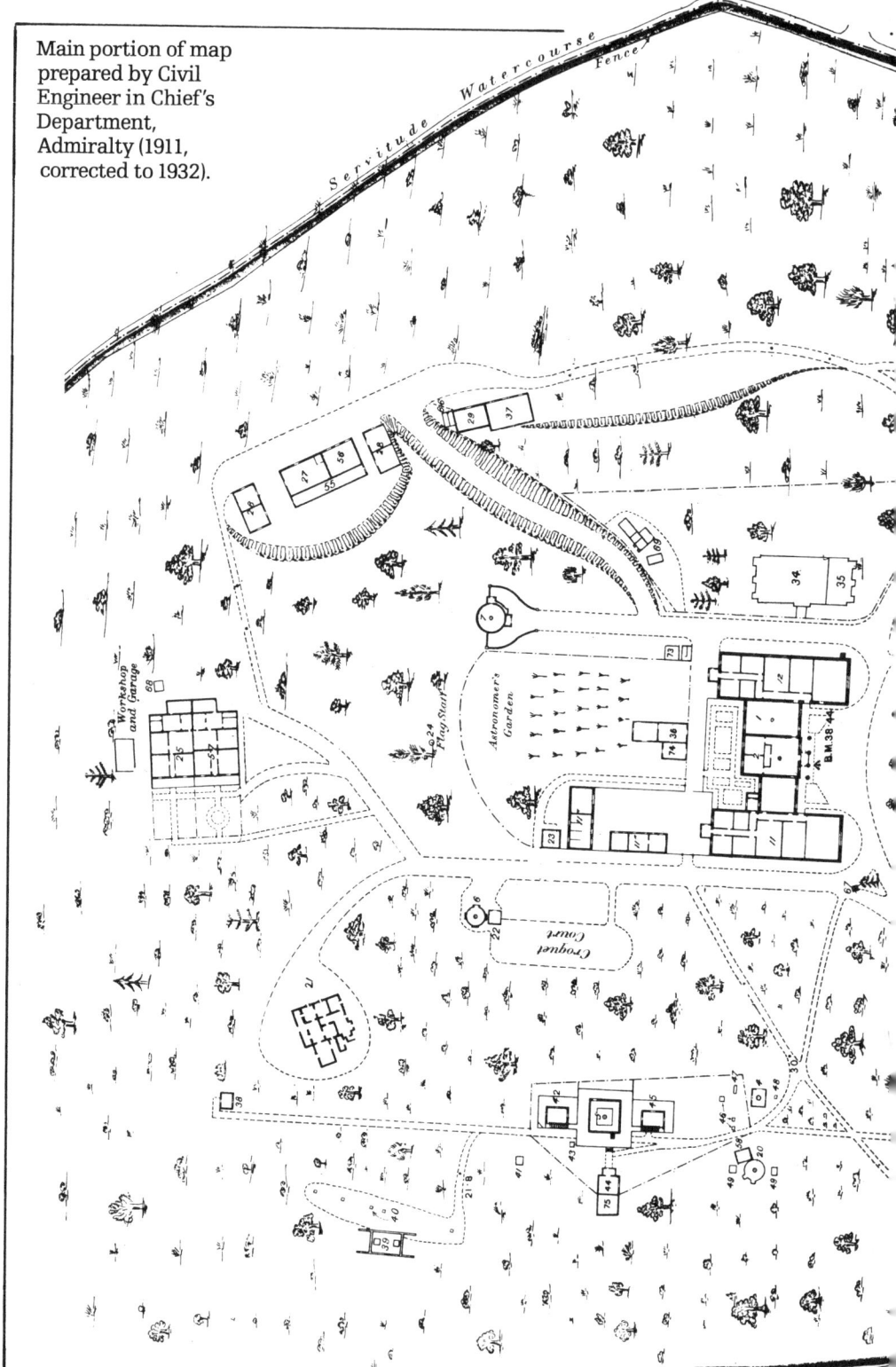

Main portion of map prepared by Civil Engineer in Chief's Department, Admiralty (1911, corrected to 1932).

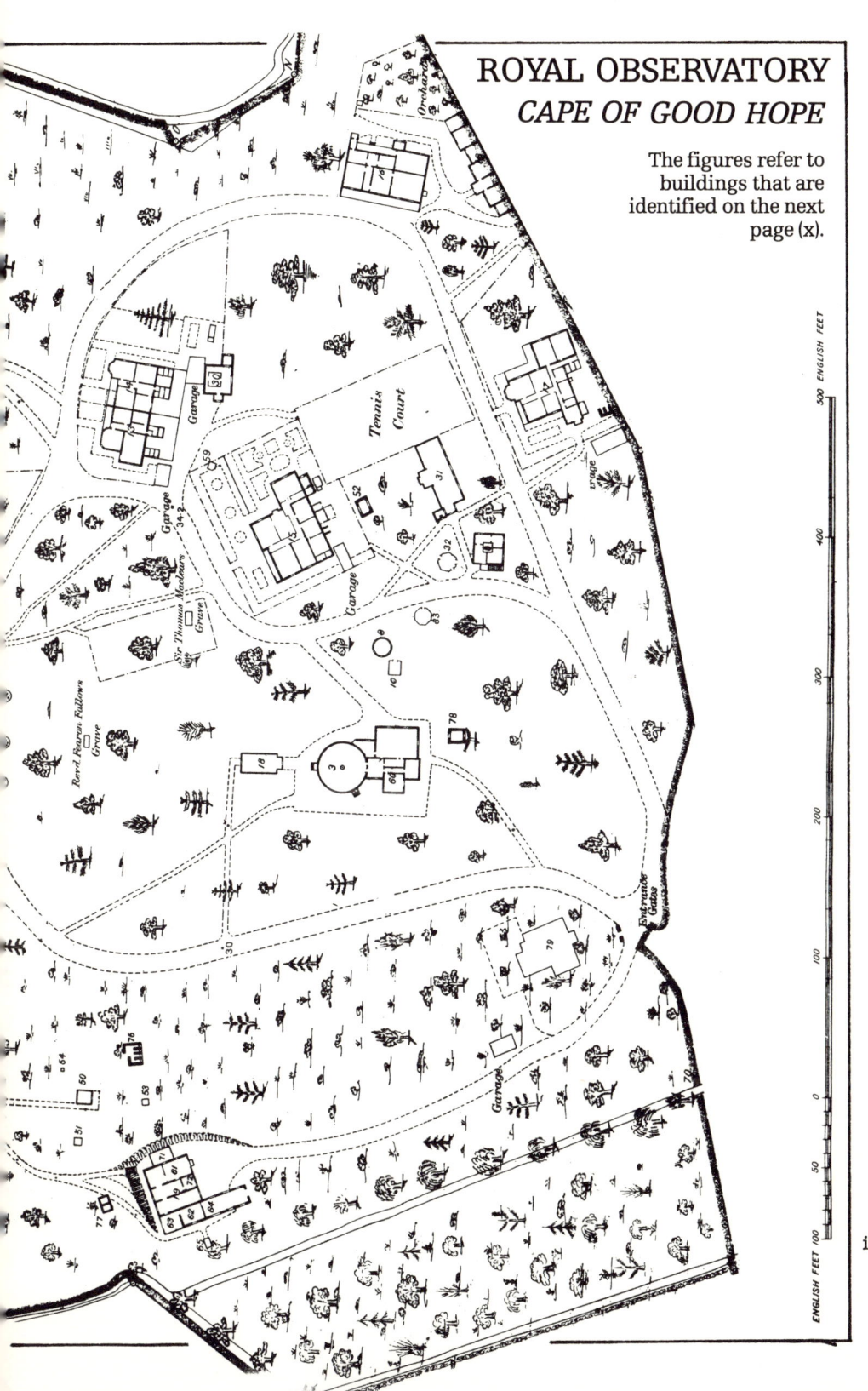

References to the figures used on the map on pages viii/ix

1 Centre of Transit Circle
2 Anemometer. Over Library
3 McClean Observatory. Centre of Dome
4 Zenith Telescope. Centre of Pier
5 Transit Circle. Centre of Pier
6 7 inch Equatorial. Centre of Dome
7 Heliometer
8 Astro-Photo. Observatory
9 6 inch Equatorial
10 Small Transit Inst. Centre.
11 H.M. Astronomer's Quarters
11a H.M. A's Stables and Servants' Quarters
12 Chief Assistant's Quarters
13 Assistants' Quarters. No. 4
14   do.   do.   No. 3
15   do.   do.   No. 6
16 Higher Grade Computer's Quarters. No. 7.
17 Assistants' Quarters. No. 5
18 Battery House
19 Engine House
20 Indian Theodolite Hut
21 Mr. Pead's House
22 Battery Hut
23 Old Time Ball
24 Flag Staff
25 Artificers' Quarters
26 Stores Nos. 1 & 2
27 Carpenter's Shop
28 Store No. 4
29 Store No. 5
30 Siderial Clock House
31 Record Room No. 2
32 Photo-Helio Hut
33 Photo-Telescope Hut
34 Offices
35 Library
36 Battery House
37 Store No. 6
38 North Mark R.T.C.
39 Site of Franklin Adams Observatory

40 Standard Lengths
41 North Mark Theodolite
42 North Collimator
43 Thermometer
44 Chronograph House
45 South Collimator
46 Rain Gauges
47 Foundation for Transit
48 Mark
49 Mark Lens
50 South Mark R.T.C.
51 South Mark Theodolite
52 Seismograph House
53 Water Tank
54 Mark Zenith Telescope
55 Paint Store. No. 3
56 Kroomens' Quarters
57 Leading Man's Quarters
58 Annex to Indian Theodolite
59 Dip House
60 Physical Laboratory
61 E.Es Store and Workshop
62 Workshop for Artificer
63 Blacksmith's Shop
64 Workshop for Optical Fitter
65 Earth Closet
66 Earth Closets
67 Thermometer
68 Coal Stores
69 Fuel Stores
70 Gas Meter
71 Coal Store
72 Store
73 Cart Shed
74 Fire Hose House (Tank over)
75 Wireless Receiving Room
76 Male Staff Latrines
77 Refuse Destructor
78 Electrical Transformer House
79 Entrance Lodge

Foreword

The Royal Observatory at the Cape of Good Hope, founded in 1820, was the first organised scientific institution to be established in South Africa. During the nineteenth century the Observatory played an influential part in Cape life: several of its Directors (namely Fallows, Maclear and Gill) were socially and politically active and the Observatory itself served as a cultural centre for Cape Town. Until the 1880's, the astronomical work of the Observatory was of a routine nature, lacking in innovation. By the turn of the century, however, the Observatory was clearly established as the leader in the southern hemisphere; equal to the best in the northern hemisphere. At the same time, Cape Town, with its expanded population and increased variety of scientific and industrial institutions, had also changed. The result was that, in the twentieth century, the Observatory no longer occupied such a special position in Cape life. Although the members of staff continued to contribute enthusiastically to community affairs, they were of diminished importance.

The account given in this book of the activities of the Observatory follows these changes of character. Throughout the nineteenth century the personality of each of the Astronomers, as well as their scientific and other contributions, is described in an individual chapter. (The first chapter provides a particularly detailed biography of the first Astronomer, Fearon Fallows, who has, in my opinion, been unjustly neglected by other writers on the history of the Observatory). In the twentieth century, on the other hand, my account of Observatory activities is condensed into one chapter; the casual reader will probably not require any more elaboration than is thereby presented.

Throughout the writing of this book I have relied solely on original sources. As a result, there are some anecdotes, related by other authors but for which there is no documentary evidence, that I have had to omit. In other cases I am sceptical. For example, one of the most commonly repeated stories about the Observatory in its early days is that obtained by Gill from a resident in Cape Town. This concerned a hippopotamus, stuck in the marsh near the Observatory, which could only be killed by shots fired through holes cut in its hide. I found this an acceptable story of Observatory life until I read an account, identical in all details as to location and modus operandi (but referring to a rhinoceros) in Van Riebeeck's Journal for 1655! I suspect that over the years, the original location 'near the mouth of the Salt River' became more conveniently 'near the new Observatory', which was later transformed to 'near the Observatory when it was new'.

In a book of this nature, that is intended to reach a wide readership, I have deliberately avoided encumbering the text with references to sources. It is my intention, at a later date, to offer more exhaustive treatment of certain aspects of the available material; this will provide the opportunity for a full list of references. The principal sources are evident from the acknowledgements given below.

In the first fifty years of its existence, the Observatory attracted the admiration of many of the artists resident in, or passing through Cape Town. Their works are used here as an iconography of the Observatory in its early years. The availability of these illustrations usefully supplements the emphasis I have given to the history of the Observatory in the nineteenth century.

I acknowledge with pleasure the generous assistance or facilities afforded me by the following individuals and institutions:

Phil Laurie, Eric Rosenthal, Rupert Hurly, Drummond Laing, Prof. R.H.Stoy, Dr Frank Bradlow, Dr D.W.Dewhirst, W.G.Tatham, J.Martin, A.Gordon-Brown; Miss M.Cartwright and Mr W.Tyrrell-Glynn of the South African Library; the Director of the Royal Greenwich Observatory; the successive Directors and Librarians of the South African Astronomical Observatory; the Librarian of the Royal Society of London; the Chairman of the Library Committee, Royal Astronomical Society; the Cambridge Observatories; the Public Record Office; The Humanities Research Centre, University of Texas; the Librarian, St John's College, Cambridge; the Jagger Library, University of Cape Town; the Assistants in the Cape Archives; the Africana Library, Johannesburg; the Durban City Library; the Royal Society of Edinburgh; Aylesbury County Record Office; the Museum for the History of Science, Oxford; the Library of Parliament, Cape Town; the National Maritime Museum and the Royal Geographical Society.

My wife, Nancy, has given invaluable aid in research and in preparation of the text, for which I have frequently given my thanks. I am most grateful to Mrs P.J.K.Dobbie for her care and patience in typing the manuscript and its preparation for the printer. I acknowledge with gratitude a subvention from the Editorial Board of the University of Cape Town which has assisted the publication of this book.

Department of Astronomy,   Brian Warner
University of Cape Town

1   Fearon Fallows
1820-1831

"The end of the eighteenth and beginning of the nineteenth centuries were remarkable for the small amount of scientific movement going on in this country, especially in its more exact departments... Mathematics were at the last gasp, and Astronomy nearly so - I mean in those members of its frame which depend upon precise measurement and systematic calculation". These words of Sir John Herschel summarized a situation of which British scientists became increasingly conscious in the second decade of the nineteenth century. In astronomy, awareness of the parlous state had at least two important results. One was initiated as described in Herschel's diary entry for 12 January 1820: "Dine at the Freemason's Tavern to meet Dr Pearson [a noted amateur astronomer] and other Gentlemen to consider of forming an Astronomical Society". This resulted in what was later to become the Royal Astronomical Society. At the same time, and perhaps involving the same people, the possibility of establishing a major observatory in the southern hemisphere was mooted. The details of these initial discussions are not known to us, but the result was that on 3 February 1820, at a meeting of the "Commissioners appointed by Act of Parliament for more effectually discovering the longitude at sea", more commonly known as the "Board of Longitude", Mr Davies Gilbert, M.P. "proposed that the Board should take into consideration the propriety of the establishment of an observatory at the Cape of Good Hope, which he observed was likely to be conducive to the improvement of astronomy". The motion was seconded by the famous botanist and explorer Sir Joseph Banks, currently in his forty-second year as President of the Royal Society. Over the following five months the Board planned the general arrangement of the Observatory and on 22 July they submitted their deliberations to the Secretary of the Board of Admiralty, John Barrow. The Admiralty supported the proposal and started negotiations with the Treasury and Colonial Office. Earl Bathurst, the Principal Secretary of State for the Colonial Department, fully concurred in the desirability of an observatory at the Cape and sent instructions to the Governor of the Cape to provide a suitable piece of land, at the expense of the Colonial Government. The

Observatory was established on 20 October 1820 by an Order in Council of His Majesty King George IV.

In setting up the Observatory at the Cape of Good Hope, the Board of Longitude envisaged an institution of similar size and standing as the famous Royal Greenwich Observatory. The Astronomer was to be appointed at the same salary (£600 per annum) as the Astronomer Royal at Greenwich; he had an assistant at £250 per annum and a labourer at £100 per annum. The title of the astronomer was never clearly specified; throughout the nineteenth century the Admiralty would in general address him as The Astronomer, or occasionally H.M. Astronomer. Some official publications appeared, however, with the ascription "Astronomer Royal at the Cape of Good Hope". Locally, he was known as the Astronomer Royal and this title was frequently appended by non-official writers from overseas. In the present century, H.M. Astronomer has been used almost invariably.

The instruments for the Cape Observatory were also intended to be as powerful as those at Greenwich. The latter establishment produced accurate positions of stars under the direction of the Astronomer Royal, John Pond. His two principal instruments had been designed and built by the foremost astronomical instrument maker of his time, Edward Troughton; these were a 10-feet Transit Instrument and a 6-feet Mural Circle. The former instrument was used, in conjunction with an astronomical clock, to measure Right Ascensions (equivalent to longitude on the celestial sphere) of stars, and the latter to measure their declinations (analogous to latitudes). Identical instruments were ordered for the Cape; construction of the Transit was entrusted to George Dollond and the Mural Circle to Thomas Jones. In fact the Mural Circle constructed by Jones was kept by Pond, and a second one ordered for the Cape, with unfortunate results as will later emerge. Troughton himself was requested to build a 25-feet Zenith Sector for the Cape Observatory (to be used for very accurate latitude measurements) but through pressure of other work, nothing ever came of it.

The Board drafted a set of instructions for the Astronomer to follow on his arrival at the Cape. His general conduct was to be governed by the following considerations:

1. In the choice of the situation for the observatory he is to bear in mind the necessity of avoiding the sandy dust which pervades many parts of the colony, and the advantage of having a bright star within a minute or two of the zenith, if possible.
2. Before the completion of the observatory, he is to employ himself in making an approximate catalogue of the Southern stars with the portable transit-instrument and equatorial which have been provided for him; and to take measures for determining the latitude of La Caille's observatory.
3. When the observatory is completed and the instruments fixed, he is to make his observations as much as possible of the same kind and in the same manner as the Greenwich observations...

1   Silhouette of Fearon Fallows

In looking around for a person suited to the task of supervising the construction and then running of the Observatory at the Cape, the Board of Longitude inevitably would have first considered Cambridge graduates: the Tripos provided the necessary mathematical training for a working astronomer. They found such a man in Fearon Fallows (Figure 1).

Fallows was born on the 4 July 1789 into a humble family in Cockermouth, Cumberland. His father, John Fallows, was a hand-loom weaver but with sufficient education to act also as clerk in the neighbouring parish of Bridekirk. John Fallows encouraged Fearon's early interests in arithmetic and geometry.

With the support of the Vicar of Bridekirk, the Revd H.A. Hervey, and an anonymous patron, Fearon was enabled in October 1809 to enter St John's College, Cambridge. He was a highly successful student and in almost any

2   An impression of the proposed observatory by the architect John Rennie

other year undoubtedly would have achieved the distinction of becoming Senior Wrangler, but he chanced to be up at the same time as J.F.W. Herschel and N. Peacock - two of the outstanding mathematicians of the nineteenth century. Herschel, son of the famous Sir William Herschel, inter alia, was destined to play a very important rôle in the development of the Royal Observatory at the Cape.

Fallows's success as Third Wrangler in 1813 resulted in appointment as a lecturer at Corpus Christi College and then a Fellowship of St John's in 1815. His prowess at mathematics led to his election as a Fellow of the Royal Society in 1820. Partly from the influence of the Vicar of Bridekirk, but no doubt principally because of the assistance it gave at Cambridge to one of humble origins, Fallows took Holy Orders, becoming a Deacon in 1815 and a Priest in 1819.

Previous commentators on the career of Fallows have thought him unversed in matters of practical astronomy until his unexpected appointment as Astronomer Royal at the Cape. He was considered to have learned his trade in a flurry of activity, prior to sailing, but surviving letters show otherwise. While at Corpus Christi, Fallows built a small reflecting telescope, grinding his own speculum metal mirror. As a Fellow of St John's, he observed the solar eclipse of 18 November 1816 from his "rooms in Bell Turret first court".

In early 1820 Fallows became disenchanted with life as a Cambridge don and hoped to set himself up in a small observatory with an independent income. In March he wrote to the Revd Hervey saying that "Many of my university acquaintances have advised me to apply for a situation at the Cape of Good Hope (viz) the direction of the observatory about to be established received no injury in the removal from the Hold to the Shore, for sailors are such rough hands that they would make no difference between a cask of herrings & the cases containing the circle & clock. As the surf runs high in the bay, the cases were again to be removed from the boat by means of a Crane at the end of the jetty adjoining the Dockyard. - They were then carried to the place appointed for their temporary reception. I fully expected that they might be easily conveyed by means of Ox-waggon to Cape Town; in this however I was deceived, for the first part of the road (about 8 miles) I found so excessively bad that it would be the height of temerity to make the attempt. - With the consent of the Commissioner I determined to reship the cases in the first vessel bound for Table Bay & as before, requested Mr Fayrer to overlook the management of putting them on board lest their places might be changed during the short voyage in order (as the Sailors say) to put the ship in better trim, - I thought it further advisable to direct Mr. F. to accompany them. ...Immediately upon my arrival in Cape Town I took lodgings for myself & family [with Carel Bestandig at 22 Grave Street - now Parliament Street], & paid my respect to the Acting Governor.... While we were in lodgings I made enquiries of the Colonial Secretary, Coll. Bird if he had received any orders, from England, for the payment of incidental expences attending the lading of the Instruments in Table Bay, their repair in case of injury (for I had no means of procuring a work Shop), the erection of a temporary Observatory, travelling &c &c &c. when to my utter astonishment he told me he had no orders of the kind. I then wished to know whether any money could be advanced on the account of the Observatory. - I was then given to understand not one penny would be allowed. Judge then (my Dr. Herschel) my distress. Conceive yourself in a far distant land, sent out under the highest patronage for the promotion of the most noble objects & an apparently insuperable bar to any success presents itself at the very onset. I cannot depict my state of mind at that time, suffice to say, that I was nearly overwhelmed with grief & disappointment. If a letter was forwarded to the Admiralty, no answer could be expected within six or seven months at the least, during which period I should be condemned to live in strenua inertia. I now expected the arrival of the ship containing the Instruments, but where could I deposit them? In none of the King's store rooms could any place be granted after repeated application. The Ship arrived & the Captain wishing to discharge his Cargo, sent me word that he would put the Cases on shore & leave them there unless I immediately hired boats & men to have them removed safely. With tears in my eyes I went to the Colonial Secretary & happening to find the President of the Burgher Senate (a most respectable Dutch gentleman) with him, I communicated the situation of the Instruments which I had brought with me from home & the great probability of them receiving great damage in landing from the Captain's threat of putting them on shore. - The President said, he thought there might be a spare room in the Granary and at Coll. Bird's urgent request, told me all the Cases should be lodged there & that I should have possession of the Key. Shortly after I hired a small house by the month with a little garden attached to it, at a most enormous rent. I pay for the house alone nearly one-fourth of my income. Servants wages too are very considerable, even slaves cannot be hired under 25 Dollars a month each, & they are a most vile, thieving set of fellows, and require more looking after than they are worth. Having got permission from the President of the Burger Senate to deposit the Cases in the Town Granary I was still haunted by the fear of the want of money. Little did I expect that the charge for Mr Fayrer's passage from Simon's Town to Table Bay would be refused to be paid by the agents of His Majesty's Government here, as I had merely directed him to abide by the Instruments & see that they were not hurt in the voyage,- and let it be borne in mind the property belonged to the King. The Captain sent me the bill of 100 Dollars, saying 'it has been refused to be discharged by Government'. Here was the beginning of my sorrows. After a long conversation with my wife, we finally agreed to live as sparingly as possible and whatever we could possibly save out of our income to apply it to the use of the temporary Observatory which I wished to get ready without delay. This plan being determined upon, I was still at a loss, how to get a place adapted for the Transit & Circle [the portable instruments]. No house in Town could be made fit for any such purpose, for suppose I could obtain permission to make an opening in the roof in the direction of the Meridian, still what could be done in case of making observations with the Alt. & Az'th Circle out of the Meridian should any circumstance occur which might render such observations necessary.;- and this seemed more than probable from the expectation of the comet of 1819 visiting us in 1822 - For some time I really thought that nothing could be done till I heard from England again. At length I discovered that Government had sent out several wooden Houses for the Settlers at Algoa Bay. I then made immediate application to Sir Rufane Donkin, who allowed me to have one of them. The wooden House was erected in my Garden and the necessary alterations made in the roof, so that I could easily take it off altogether when occasion required. A small brick pillar was built for supporting the Transit and I caused to be fixed a huge stone of a Ton & a half weight, in the ground for bearing the Circle & its frame. The Clock was carefully placed between the two instruments. All the expences which have accumulated since the arrival of the ship to the moment of writing this letter for the use of the Observatory have been paid out of my own pocket, when God knows how ill I can spare the money. The Case containing the Circle being very large & unwieldy, I was much afraid lest it might have suffered injury. I was not mistaken in my fears for almost all the instruments had received some damage. The Transit was little worse so that it was ready for observation in a short time.

3   Garden Rozenhof by Rev. John Campbell

The 1820 Settlers' hut that Fallows received from Admiralty stores in October 1821, was erected in the garden of 13 Kloof Street*, a property owned by Arend Josias van Breda and known as Garden Rozenhof (Figure 3). There he set to work with his portable instruments to prepare a preliminary catalogue of positions of the brighter southern stars from which he could later select stars to be measured when the Observatory was completed.

The Acting Governor, Sir Rufane Donkin, visited two or three times a week to watch progress. When the Governor, Lord Charles Somerset, returned to the Cape on 30 November 1821 he opposed the actions of Donkin and ostracised his friends, who included Colonel Bird and Fallows. Fallows committed "a sin not to be forgiven" when he was reported to have paid his respects to Donkin as the latter embarked for England.

On 6 December 1822 Fallows's observing book comments "Changed my Residence and therefore obliged to fix the observatory again". He had in some way fallen out with Van Breda; the only cause that has come down to us is that Van Breda (whose house adjoined that of Fallows) "one day took offence at Mr Fallows looking into Breda's backyard from the top of the house, Breda contending that Mr F. came to the Colony for the sole purpose of looking upwards and not downwards".

Fallows removed to Garden Zorg en Lust, belonging to Heinrich Pieter Moller, on a site now occupied by the Ladies' Christian Home. There he continued his preliminary observations, which concluded with the star catalogue that in June 1823 he communicated for publication in the Philosophical Transactions of the Royal Society. About this same time, Fallows commenced a time service for ships in Table Bay: he shone an Argand lamp in the evening and doused it at a pre-arranged time.

From the time of his arrival in Cape Town, Fallows actively sought a suitable site for the intended Observatory. On explaining that he wanted to establish the Observatory on a hill, the Colonial Government, "considering that proximity to the stars was a sine qua non", offered him a site on Table Mountain! His initial report, sent to Sir John Barrow (the Secretary of the Admiralty, who had himself resided at the Cape from 1796-1802) on 5 September 1821 states that "I am now happy to say that from a careful examination of the country for twenty miles around, the spot (Tiger Hill) which you suggested to me on my departure from England appears the most eligible of any within the circuit that I have lately traversed". He "constantly bore in mind the necessity of avoiding Sandy dust, which would be highly prejudicial to the instruments, but indeed the difficulty of escaping it is so great that I would not trust merely to the reports of the neighbouring Boors [sic] but determined to examine carefully the soil to see if any particles of the sand prevaded [sic] it".

In selecting Tygerberg he was, however "concerned to state that no water can be got and no grass will grow on the top or near the top of Tiger Hill so that I am afraid I shall be in rather a deplorable condition when I fix my residence there particularly from want of water".

On 8 March 1822 Fallows wrote to the Admiralty to say that he had changed his mind and asked to be excused for his earlier recommendation of Tygerberg "since I had not been given to understand at that time, that mountain mists were very prevalent in this Colony. My attention was first drawn to this circumstance by a conversation which I had with our late acting Governor Sir Rufane Donkin who pointed out the propriety of carefully watching their progress during the summer months". He further explained, in a letter to Herschel, that "I made particular enquiries amongst the Dutch Boors who live in decent farm houses scattered round the base of the Hill. From these kind and hospitable people I found that my suspicions were correct, (viz) that the mists which I observed collected up the summit in the evening were not dissipated before one or two o'Clock in the morning". It was well for the future of the Royal Observatory that Fallows did abandon all thoughts of this location, which Herschel many years later, after having himself resided at the Cape, was to describe as "a most strange and unaccountable one to fix upon".

Anticipating his conclusion about Tygerberg, in early February Fallows had taken his "horse, a sextant and a bearing compass and traversed almost every inch of ground for forty or fifty miles every way round Cape Town. The result of the examination was, that no spot possessed any advantage, which could not be obtained even to a greater degree in the immediate vicinity of Cape Town... With this view, I began to examine the neighbourhood of Cape Town from Wynberg towards the North to Table Bay. ...In the space of a few days I was at last fortunate enough in finding a place which combined as many advantages as could be expected... Lest the distant sand might, during the summer months, be felt at this place I went several times for the express purpose of putting it to the test when the wind was so strong as to render riding on Horseback exceedingly dangerous, - once I was completely blown from my horse. The result was very satisfactory:- no minute particles of sand could be perceived. A sufficient supply of water is obtained with great ease as two small rivers run within a short distance".

The site chosen by Fallows was near the confluence of the Salt and Liesbeek rivers, "contiguous to respectable Farm Houses where the usual necessaries of life can be easily purchased. The distance to Cape Town is nearly three miles, the road very good - were a small wooden bridge erected over Liesbeek's river which at times is hardly fordable, it would secure an easy intercourse with Town - a point of the utmost consequence when medical assistance might be required". The low hill, covered with brushwood, was an outcrop of "whinstone", covered with clay. One report states that the site was used as a burial ground for slaves. The accumulation of snakes in this uncultivated spot resulted in its local name of "Hele-Slang" or "Slangkop".

Having settled on a site, it only remained for the Colonial Government to acquire the land for the Admiralty, and for the plans of the building to arrive; then Fallows could start construction. To his frustration, nothing happened for nearly two years. Although the Warrant for building arrived at Simon's Town Naval Yard in April 1823, and Fallows frequently wrote to complain that time was being wasted, the building plans were not received until 16 December 1824. The cause of the delay was two-fold. In the first place, in April 1822 Fallows had been seriously ill, caused in part by his trip into the interior and in part by long night exposure in his temporary observatory. He suffered a relapse later in the year. As he explained to his father-in-law in September 1823, "the Plan has not yet come to hand owing to my illness as the Admiralty had every reason to expect from the reports of my health that I must be obliged to return to England". The rest of the delay appears to have arisen from incredible inefficiency in the Admiralty Office: having shelved the plans, they were forgotten and then could not be found. The six months round trip of communications also played a part here; an entry in the Admiralty Minutes for 5 October 1824 stated "referred to Mr Barrow's letter of 25 December last, respecting Plan for Observatory at the Cape of Good Hope which it appears had not reached the Cape on July 18 last, and desired to state cause of delay". It was this enquiry that finally sent the plans on their way. Immediately prior to this, however, the drawings had been considerably modified; the set sent out to

4   Redesigned appearance of the Observatory

the Cape carries the date 1 September 1824. The changed appearance of the proposed building is seen in Figure 4. The arrival of the plans prompted the Governor to issue the grant of land required for the Observatory. Part of the land already belonged to the Colonial Government, but the majority was owned by Cornelis Mostert. After many negotiations, Mostert had been persuaded to cede to Government his "One Morge, Fifty Square Roods, Thirtytwo ditto Feet, and Fortytwo ditto Inches of Land", in return for which a piece of land of over 31 Morgen which he previously held in Quitrent was given to him Freehold.

Before following the progress of building in 1825, we look back over Fallow's life since he arrived in August 1821. It had been a period of considerable trials, especially for a person of his naive and unwordly nature.

On the personal side, the Fallows' son, John William, born on 19 December 1822, had lived only until 31 January. Mary Anne Fallows subsequently had several miscarriages.

Fallows was also unfortunate with his servants and assistants. His Assistant Fayrer had emerged as a lazy and insolent drunkard. On 13 May 1822 he married the Fallows' maid, Sarah Bootle, Fallows explaining in a letter to the Revd Hervey that "as soon as she thought she was going to make a good match, she behaved very impertinently to Mary. She is very fond of the bottle and many times she was in such a state of intoxication as to be carried to bed... Mary told me she would have no intercourse with such a Woman and of course I am under the necessity of parting with Mr Fayrer. He is going to set up for himself as watchmaker". Fayrer in fact was demoted to Labourer and paid a retainer of £100 per annum, but was only occasionally called upon to clean or repair the instruments at the Observatory. On 16 November 1822 he advertised in the Government Gazette that he had taken over the business of Mr Wilson and pointed out that he

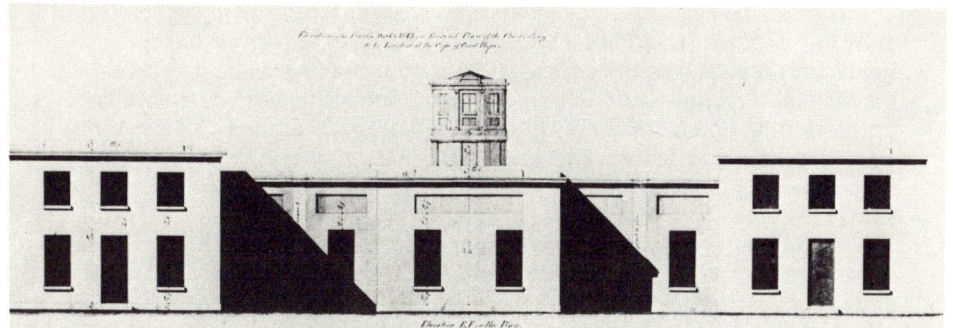

had been trained by Edward Troughton. His notice ends with the statement "His Majesty's Astronomer has kindly notified his intention of allowing Mr J.F. (to the exclusion of others), the true Solar Time". Fallows's award of the exclusive franchise of real time shows his interest in Fayrer's continued well-being.

Fayrer's sister also embarrassed the Fallows, Edward Troughton writing euphemistically to say "An unexpected event which has happened at the Cape of Good Hope, seems to render it eligible that Betsy Fayrer should fourthwith [sic] return to England".

The strongest shock, however, to Fallows's belief in human nature was the result of employing the Revd Patrick Scully. Scully had arrived in Cape Town on 1 January 1820 to act as the Colony's first Catholic Chaplain. In January 1821 Donkin provided Scully with a modest salary but this was withdrawn immediately on Somerset's return. Fallows appointed him to the vacant position of labourer in November 1822. In fact, Scully was well educated and better suited than Fayrer to the observing and computations required of him; he was promoted to Assistant on Fayrer's demotion. Fallows wrote several letters to the Admiralty with glowing praise of Scully's abilities, and there is no doubt that Scully contributed a great deal to the welfare of both Fallows and the temporary observatory during this period.

Then came the shock which, at this distance in time, can be plainly stated in Fallows's own words (of 17 July 1824) to Barrow: "I am under the painful necessity of communicating through your medium to my Lords Commissioners of the Admiralty the sudden and abrupt departure of the Revd Mr Scully from this Colony, which took place on Sunday last... Unfortunately for the man, I was compelled to become an eye witness of his improprieties with a young house-maid, about seventeen years of age, the daughter of a Settler, under my own roof. Whatever might have been the impetuosity of his passion such acts when an inmate in my house could not be passed over without severe animadversion".

Fallows's humane character shines strongly through this episode. Despite his indignation and bruised sense of propriety he wanted to feel absolutely sure that he was not acting with prejudice and accordingly submitted the facts of the case to the Governor, Lord Charles Somerset, and to one of the visiting Commissioners of Inquiry. Fallows, in informing the Admiralty of this, nevertheless requested that Scully's salary should continue for six months in order to help him settle again in England. This the Admiralty refused.

Despite the justification of the dismissal, Fallows was promptly ostracised by the Catholic community. His difficulties were compounded when he claimed moral lapses in a prominent member of another church. Apparently believing that if Fallows continued with his over-zealous application of moral rectitude, the Colony would be depleted of its clerics, Somerset brought an action of defamation of character against him. Fallows, however, was not to be intimidated and stood his ground. Somerset dropped the issue, thereby making Fallows a hero in some quarters, but undoubtedly losing him many friends in others.

Lest it be thought that Fallows's life during this period was one of unrelieved misery we interpolate a few examples of his interests and activities which would have relieved the torments of his professional life. Fallows was possessed of a strong constitution, described by a contemporary as "robust and somewhat corpulent" - in a letter to Herschel he mentions having walked from Cambridge to London in fourteen hours. Writing to Mrs Hervey he says "We are both the most noted riders on Horseback in Town - we think nothing of 20 or 30 miles, and certainly upon an average we ride a dozen miles every day". In March 1824 he reported that "... we have just returned from a long journey into the Interior of this Colony. We had a large party chiefly consisting of Gentlemen with the wifes [sic] belonging to the King's Dockyard at Simon's Town". In the same letter he states "The eldest son of the King of the Caffers and his Prime Minister dined with us lately. I had a large party of the officers in the Garrison to meet them".

He ascended Table Mountain, measured its height with the aid of a barometer, and collected flowers, bulbs and birds' nests which he packed off to friends in England.

His clerical interests were at first actively pursued, but in July 1823 he reports that "I am now doing duty at the Barrack Chapel as Acting Chaplain to the Forces, not receiving one penny of pay. Since my arrival in this Colony hardly a Sunday has passed without being obliged to take the duty of some lazy parson or one indisposed. I have come to the conclusion as these persons are abundantly well paid for doing very little to give up the clerical Character during the remainder of my residence here". He did, however, become a member of the Committee set up in May 1824 to build an English Church (later successfully erected as St George's Church).

Of the many amusing and perceptive descriptions of life in Cape Town contained in Fallows's personal letters, we have space here only for the following: "The young ladies in Cape Town go off slowly; they exhibit themselves every fine evening upon the Stoops before the houses. Perhaps the play She Stoops to Conquer would be apropos to these darling dutch belles".

To return to Observatory matters, Fallows was expecting to supervise the erection of the building himself and was therefore "determined to make myself acquainted with all the technical terms of Masonry, Carpentry, etc. as well as of the quality of the different materials..." The stormy winter of 1822 gave him first-hand experience of the quality of Cape building practices: "Every House has suffered more or less from the long continuance of rain - yesterday evening part of my House fell in with a dreadful crash, fortunately none of us were hurt, nor have we lost any thing of value. In examining the broken walls I find that the bricks have become mere rubbish by the great absorption of moisture". This was a common problem; only three years before the Governor's residence "Newlands House" had partly collapsed as a result of the poor walling materials and in 1824 Lady Somerset was nearly killed when the ceiling fell down.

With the aid of his freshly acquired technical jargon, and the assistance of William Pennell, the Naval Storekeeper at Simon's Town, Fallows drew up specifications for the building and the following advertisement was inserted in the Cape Town Gazette and African Advertiser on 29 January and 5 February, 1825:

ROYAL OBSERVATORY

Notice is hereby given to such Persons as may be willing to contract for the BUILDING of the ROYAL OBSERVATORY upon the site fixed on, between the Liesbeeks and Zwart Rivers, contiguous to the Farm of Mr MOSTERT, that proposals for the same will be received by the respective officers of the Naval Department at Simon's Town, on Monday the 13th of February next, at noon. The conditions of the Contract, with the specifications of the Materials to be used in the Building, may be seen, and any further information obtained, on application to the Rev FEARON FALLOWS, His Majesty's Astronomer, Garden Zorg en Lust, Cape Town, or at the Naval Office, Simon's Town.

No Proposals will be attended to, but from Persons fully competent to the execution of the Work, and who can provide the most satisfactory security for the due fulfilment of the Contract.

Simon's Town, Jan. 28, 1825.

W. PENNELL
Naval Officer

Fallows reported that "From the Number of Persons who daily visited me from six in the morning, to ten at night, I was led to the belief that many Tenders would be offered; in this, however, I was mistaken, for at the appointed time for receiving these Tenders, only three were presented, and what is remarkable we found only one individual (Mr Cannon of Cape Town) that seemed to be at all qualified for so large an undertaking as the Erection of the observatory".

John Cannon owned a Furniture and Ironmongery Warehouse at 1, Market Square, and a timber yard in Hottentot Square. He was one of the Cape's leading builders. Cannon's tender was accepted and work started immediately on clearing the site and digging the foundations. The hill lived up to its name and "when the workmen were clearing away for the building they destroyed from 70 to 100 snakes". Fallows reported that "While preparations were making for digging the foundations, I selected a spot on the Site where the large Transit [telescope] would hereafter be placed, and having built a small pillar there for supporting my Portable Transit, I took it out and soon obtained the approximate South point by observations upon the star α Octantis... Afterwards for several successive nights, by observations on high and low Greenwich stars, I obtained my meridian line very exactly. This being done, the lines of building as marked in the Plan were easily set off to the utmost possible accuracy".

From this time, Fallows frequently resided on the site in a tent, "fitted up with a small bed and some home comforts".

If construction had been carried out according to the specifications, the Observatory would not have lasted until the present day. In his anxiety to avoid Cape bricks, Fallows had instructed "that the Walls above the Foundations should be built with Stone laid in Clay and plastered over with Shell Lime", this being the superior mode of construction at the Cape. The Admiralty, however, must have been well-informed in these matters and, unbeknown to anyone at the Cape, a Clerk-of-Works had been appointed and was sailing to the rescue. John Skirrow arrived in Table Bay on 22 February and went early the next morning to visit Fallows on the building site; the latter was pleasantly surprised by the arrival of this trained civil engineer and architect who was to relieve him of the responsibility of the construction. Skirrow at once detected the inadequacies of the specifications, and drew up a new set, in the mean time suspending the signing of the Contract.

At this point a brief description of the Observatory is required. The general plan of the ground floor is evident from Figure 5. Built in a symmetrical form, the double-storeyed wings provided accommodation for the Astronomer and for his Assistant. The central room was originally designed with a high dome (Figure 2) intended permanently to accommodate the Zenith Sector. This tall hemi-elliptical dome was replaced in the September 1824 modifications by an octagonal wooden lantern (Figure 4). The outer rooms held the 10-feet Transit Instrument and a 6-feet Mural Circle. The telescopes looked out of the building through openings known as "chases" which could be closed with counterweighted doors operated by ropes and pulleys from inside the rooms. Originally, the Astronomer was intended to occupy the East Wing, next to the Transit, but Mrs Fallows, preferring

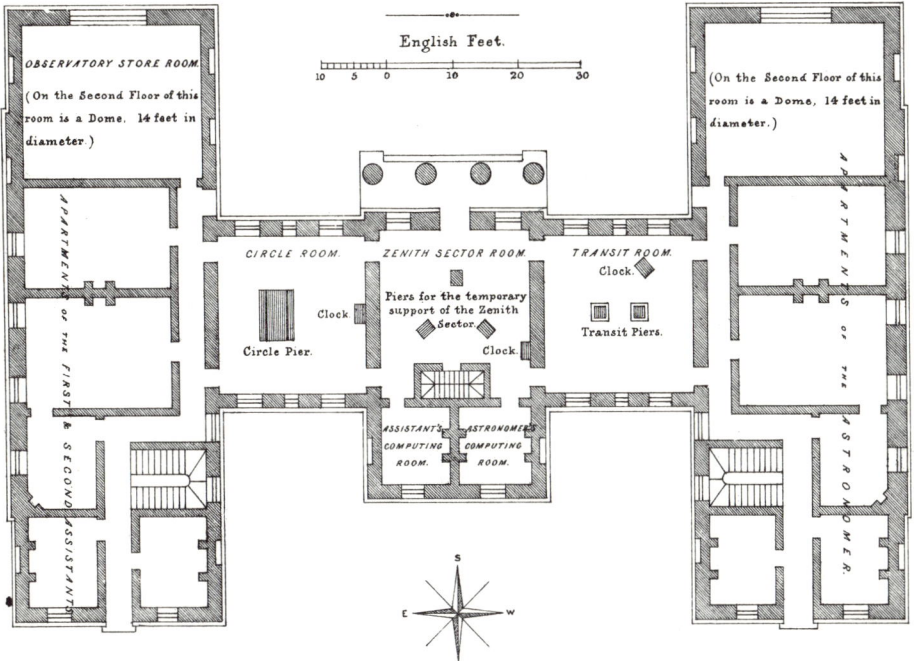

5 Ground Plan of the main building

the view of Devil's Peak, insisted that they occupy the West Wing, and the Transit was consequently erected in the west room.

The upper floors of the Wings held more residential space, and gave access to the domes on the southern extremities of the residential Wings. Several of the windows (Figure 5) were false, arising from an incorrect assumption on the part of the architect that a window tax was applied at the Cape.

The front of the building is dominated by an accurate reconstruction of the facade of a Greek temple with four Doric columns.

The front of the Observatory faces south, just as it would do in the northern hemisphere, and this has led many to believe that a mistake was made during its erection. As we have seen, Fallows laid out and had overseen the digging of the footings before Skirrow arrived. Skirrow's letters to the Navy Board accept the footings as satisfactory; the surviving copies of John Rennie's plans, dated 1 March 1821, have no north direction indicated on them, but Skirrow would undoubtedly have consulted with the Admiralty architect (John Rennie's son) before leaving England and would have known his intentions. Professor Lewcock has pointed out that contemporary buildings in other British southern colonies were similarly oriented, the purpose being to keep them cool in the hotter climates.

Skirrow was unimpressed with the quality of the workmen that he had to supervise, stating that "The Workmen consist of Malays, Africans and the refuse of the Workmen of Europe and are generally speaking the most idle and unprincipled set of men I ever witnessed with the exception of the Carpenters and Joiners, who appear to be very little inferior to those in England".

Both Skirrow and Fallows wanted the outer walls of the Observatory to be faced with "wrought stone". Earlier, Fallows had gone to considerable trouble to search for suitable building stone, reporting that "Previously to the arrival of the Plan I had made two journies to various parts of the Interior:- first, upwards of six hundred miles by the way of Tulbach [sic]; the second, along the Western Coast about four hundred miles, expressly in search of a kind of stone which might be easily faced". Although he found suitable stone near Saldanha Bay and Tulbagh, "the expense of Carriage, from the high price of labour, and bad roads, was such, as to induce me to give up the scheme". Skirrow inspected the local quarries in Cape Town and agreed with Fallows that their product was satisfactory for building, but was too hard to dress and therefore could not be used for that purpose, particularly because there were "only two or three stone Masons in the Colony". Consequently Skirrow wrote to the Admiralty and received permission to build the walls of rough stone, set in mortar, the outsides to be covered with cement, sanded (to simulate stone) and painted. For the same reason, the fluted columns of the portico were carved from wood instead of stone. The absence of a damp course gave much trouble in the 1940's. On removing some of the old plaster it was found that soft Cape bricks had been used around the windows and that the wall contained substantial cavities.

Apart from the foundations, which appear to have made use of stone from the quarry on Lion's Rump, the walls were constructed entirely of stone blasted from a quarry on site. By 18 May the foundations were finished, having required $769\frac{1}{2}$ cubic yards of digging, and the use of 11 138 cubic feet of stone. The foundations were then covered until the winter rains had diminished; work on the joinery for the window and door frames continued during the winter in Cannon's workshop.

On 12 August the following advertisement appeared in the Gazette: "MASONS WANTED by the 1st September next, sixty good Masons, and as many Labourers, to work at the Royal Observatory; likewise, thirty strong Slave Boys by the month - their Masters to find them in victuals. JOHN CANNON". Such a requirement exhausted the possibilities of qualified labour in Cape Town; Cannon had to make do with what he could get, which led to difficulties. Fallows complained that "No sooner had the work commenced, than we found such a system of plunder carried on... that it became quite unsafe to trust oneself alone without being well armed. Neither Mr Skirrow, Mr Cannon or myself durst venture to remain upon the ground after the dusk of the evening, except at the hazard of our lives. I was often compelled to be there during the night to see if the meridian line was preserved:- my situation would have been dangerous indeed had I not protected myself by fire arms and my excellent dogs. Moreover, I daily received complaints from the neighbouring Farmers of the devastation made on their property by the workmen...".

An application was made to the Governor, who agreed to "a Guard consisting of a Corporal and nine privates to be always resident upon the site". John Cannon built a guardhouse for them. After this there was no pilfering, but they could do little about "the establishment of small Brandy and Gin shops contiguous to the site" until Fallows brought in the Civil Magistrate to punish offenders. The site was then considered completely safe, and Skirrow built himself a small cottage within its boundaries, in which he resided for the next two years.

Were it not for an extraordinary piece of luck, they would have been hard put to find timber adequate for the constructional work: "A short time before the commencement of the Burmese War, a ship laden with Teak-wood from Rangoon arrived in Table Bay; its Cargo being consigned to a merchant of this Town. This Teak was of very superior quality... The question, now, was, how to procure this Wood without exciting any suspicions that we should be in want of a large quantity of it. There was no other Teak in the Colony and from the prospect of affairs in India no likelihood of any future importation till the War ceased; I therefore kept a profound silence respecting it... I knew well that if the slightest suspicion had existed on the part of the possessor of the Wood, that we wanted so large a supply of it, it would have risen to an enormous price... Mr Cannon by some means or other purchased the Timber at a reasonable price and bound himself to use it in the observatory". This astute but devious procedure provided the magnificent wood from which the Observatory joinery was prepared.

By the end of 1825 the walls were carried up to the height of the external cornice and most of the timber beams had been installed. At the end of March 1826 all the stone work was completed and the woodwork of the roof was almost finished. At this time it was intended that work should again be halted for the winter, but, the whole building being covered by a painted ship's sail obtained from Simon's Town, it was found possible to continue with the inside plastering and some of the joinery. Despite another heavy winter, no damage was done to the walls, and the canvas roof held without a leak.

Lead for the roof arrived from England in August 1826. This expensive roofing material had been deemed necessary by Skirrow because of the impossibility of otherwise constructing leak-proof horizontal roofs at the Cape.

The building continued steadily until the end of 1827, when everything was completed except for the floors in the three observing rooms, and the two domes which had not arrived from England. The floors remained unfinished because heavy stone piers had to be constructed on which the principal instruments would be erected. Provision of these piers now led to a serious delay. Work on the piers, obtained from a "Quarry on the side of Table Mountain belonging to J. Ingram [of Zonnebloem]", had started on 19 February 1827, but progress was very slow "from the extreme hardness of the Stone of which they are making and also from the great deficiency of good Masons in the Colony". The pier for the Mural Circle contained only four blocks of stone, the largest weighing eleven tons. This was heavier than any ox cart could carry, and the inhabitants of Cape Town were treated to the spectacle of this huge block being warped like a ship, using anchors and windlasses, over the road from Zonnebloem to the Observatory. The journey took three weeks!

On 1 January 1828 the building was completed sufficiently for the Fallows to take up occupation. Before describing the final phase of Fallows's life at the Observatory, we review some of the events concomitant with the building of the Observatory.

As a result of Scully's dismissal a new Assistant was required. A Captain William Ronald had recently applied for a position as Assistant at the Royal Greenwich Observatory, and Pond, the Astronomer Royal, considered him to be suitable for the Cape appointment, which was approved by the Admiralty on 1 December 1824. However, Ronald did not immediately leave for the Cape, but was detained in London to inspect the Transit Instrument and Mural Circle, still under construction for the Cape Observatory, and to become familiar with their use by acquiring experience at the Greenwich Observatory. He was further delayed when it was decided that he should accompany the instruments on their journey to the Cape, and in consequence did not arrive at the Cape until 19 November 1826.

Off-loading the cases of instruments from the ship (Susannah) was not a trivial operation and a minor accident occurred which caused Fallows to write a detailed report. He pointed out that "To land the Transit and Mural upon the Beach was utterly impossible, and the present state of the Jetty is such as to excite considerable alarm when any heavy weight is to be raised upon it. We therefore lashed all the Cranes to each other by strong ropes and the Block which was attached to the large Cases, was slung between two of the Cranes so as to divide the weight between them. ... I must remark that on one side of the lower edge of the Mural Case, the wood was slightly chipped which indicated a blow that it had received before it was lifted upon the Jetty. Capt Ronald informed me that this happened from the Tackle giving way in raising the Case from the Hold to the Deck. From the manner in which the Mural is packed I should not apprehend the slightest damage to the Circle". This apparently minor incident will appear magnified in the later history of the Observatory.

The instruments were stored in Cape Town until a room in the East Wing of the Observatory was ready to receive them. Fallows anticipated that "We shall have no little difficulty in conveying the Mural to the Site (about four miles) on account of the Enormous weight of the Case, I purpose to have it borne by relays of Coolies, and whenever there may be a necessity of resting it, to place beds immediately under the Case, lest any accident should occur". This was eventually carried out on 7 June 1827; 98 labourers were employed at 3/6^d each.

While the Observatory was under construction, Fallows busied himself with a compound pendulum that Captain Ronald had brought from England. He built two small piers about fifty yards south-east of the East Wing and put his 1820 Settlers' hut over them. On one pier he set his portable transit, with a clock close to it, and on the other he erected the pendulum stand. By timing the swings of the pendulum, with the aid of his clock which could be kept in good time by observations of stars with the transit, Fallows was able to measure the acceleration due to gravity at the Cape. Ronald had previously swung the pendulum in London. The results of these measurements could be used to deduce the shape of the Earth. Fallows's results appeared in the Philosophical Transactions for 1830; apart from his short catalogue of approximate star positions, it was the only substantial paper he was destined to publish. His results have been adequately verified by later measurements.

A constant source of irritation throughout this period was the Admiralty's insistence on economy. About £40 000 had originally been granted, which would have been sufficient for the instruments, the main building, several auxiliary buildings, furniture, etc. When the Whigs came to power in 1827 they rescinded the financial agreement and recovered £10 000 not yet committed. A later resident at the Observatory, Piazzi Smyth, explained "The outhouses, offices etc. were never completed or even begun: the supply of money was suddenly cut off, as was said by reason of a change of Ministry; & there the Obs^y, the H-building, was left, by itself, finished within itself to admiration, but only a part of the original design; the dirty black flea-y servants were never intended to go into the beautiful rooms of the wings so exquisitely fitted up; there was to have been a range of low outhouses just below the crest of the hill for them, & for the workshops, carpenters, & instrument makers, & for horses and carts so necessary in an isolated situation. The ground too was to have been in some little degree smoothed & enclosed, & a road to the Obs^y was to have been made in connection with Cape Town. Thus the Obs^y building appeared accidentally dropped from the clouds in a rough wilderness, without any sort of enclosure, & in a manner in the middle of a highway, for when the marsh below was very full of water in the winter, the waggons & cattle used to come over the hill, grazing the corner of the building. There was no road to Cape Town, other than by wading through the river & crossing a piece of marshy ground... Then as a substitute for the stabling, after the harlequin wave of the wand had been performed, there were found [in 1834] amongst the rubbish N.W. of the house about 50 or 100 feet from it, still standing, a portable wooden settler's hut used by the workmen as a tool house, & a plank built house covered with canvas employed as the soldier's guard house, these were turned into the Astronomer's stable & outhouse, the black fellows he was obliged to admit into the wing with himself. The assistant Capt Ronald, having no stable at all, built one for himself under the hill [to the north-east]".

Fallows received several strictures on expenditure and rebuffs in attempts to improve the amenities. He had wisely secured (at no cost) a considerable amount of Government land surrounding the Observatory, intending to prevent development of the land and so preserve the quality of the site. He requested the Admiralty to allow him to plant trees and hedges on the Observatory ground but was told that in the Lord High Admiral's opinion "if you have any desire to beautify the ground it must be done at your own expense, and His Royal Highness desires you will not incur any kind of expense nor purchase any ground without his express authority".

Tradition has it that, as a result of this rebuff, Fallows gave private lessons to the children of neighbouring farmers and was paid in loads of topsoil. There is no documented evidence for this story and in any case there was fertile soil on the site; what was lacking was adequate irrigation.

The unsympathetic response was a result of an incident that had angered the Admiralty. Fallows had pointed out that the East Wing was suitable only for one family - that of the Assistant - and inquired what was to be done to house the Labourer? He received the reply that the Assistant (Capt Ronald) "is to occupy the East Wing, and the Labourer is to be provided for elsewhere". However, by this time it had also been made clear that no outhouses would be forthcoming, so Fallows naively took the Admiralty's reply as authority to purchase and promptly acquired "Klerk's Kraal" for £487.10.0. Klerk's estate adjoined the Observatory property to the northeast and included a humble cottage. Fayrer gladly came to live in it. Presented with the fait accompli, the Admiralty grudgingly sanctioned the purchase, but from this date their letters increasingly refused Fallows's requests and demanded explanations for what little expenditure he did incur.

In a private letter, Thomas Maclear (whom we will meet in Chapter 3) said of Fallows: "His special correspondence was carried on seemingly on any scrap of paper that came to hand, until 1829 when he received a rap across the knuckles from Mr Croker (Secretary to the Admiralty). Even after this for a time their composition was colloquial and were probably very amusing to the clerks at the Admiralty. To these circumstances perhaps may be traced the stringency of some of their Lordships letters".

Fallows's frustrations at the treatment he was receiving both at home and abroad were increased by the knowledge that he had been in the Colony for seven years and still had not started serious observing. He had expected to be the first to use large astronomical instruments in the Southern hemisphere, but the delay had resulted in his losing pride of place to Sir Thomas Brisbane's observatory at Paramatta, New South Wales, which began work in 1823. The observer, James Dunlop, received the Gold Medal of the Royal Astronomical Society in 1828 for his Catalogue of Southern Stars.

During 1826 the quality of construction at the Observatory had been brought to the attention of the Acting Governor, Sir Richard Bourke, who wrote to the Secretary to the Colonies, Lord Bathurst, pointing out "the want of a Civil Engineer and Architect" in the Colony and proposing Skirrow. Although Skirrow was not officially appointed to these positions (and also Superintendent of the Cape Town Waterworks) until the end of 1828, he vacated his cottage on the Observatory site late in 1827, resided in Cape Town, and became increasingly involved in Colonial matters.* As a result, work on completing the Observatory, and in particular the instrument piers, came almost to a halt. Fallows received much criticism from England for the paucity of progress, which he bore with fortitude.

In October 1828 the piers were at last ready to receive their respective instruments. The building was also complete except for the domes which had yet to arrive from England. When construction had started, the laying of the first stone was awarded no official ceremony, presumably because at this time Fallows and the Governor (Somerset) were not on speaking terms. The arrival of the new Governor, Sir Lowry Cole, in September 1828 coincided with the final stages of construction of the Observatory, and Fallows decided to make use of this opportunity. On 29 October 1828 the Governor was present at the laying of the final stone of the Mural Circle pier, and to commemorate this event Fallows inserted the following note into a cavity in the stone:

Present at the laying of this Stone	October 29th 1828
Mrs Fallows	Manuel John Johnson
Mrs Ronald	John Skirrow
Reverend Fearon Fallows	Sir Laury Cole (lately arrived Governor)
Captain Ronald	John Bell, Colonial Secretary

Of those present, only Manuel Johnson requires additional explanation. He was a Lieutenant in the St Helena Artillery and had been appointed by the East India Company to be in charge of the Observatory on St Helena. To gain experience, he visited Fallows from 29 December 1825 until 5 March 1826, while the Cape Observatory was under construction, and again from 12 September 1828 until 7 March 1829 when the instruments were going into operation. During this latter period he assisted in Fallows's pendulum experiments. He produced a valuable catalogue of southern stars which earned

*Skirrow supervised the erection of a number of buildings in Cape Town, including St George's Church, in which was propagated the neoclassical design first introduced at the Observatory. He died in 1847.

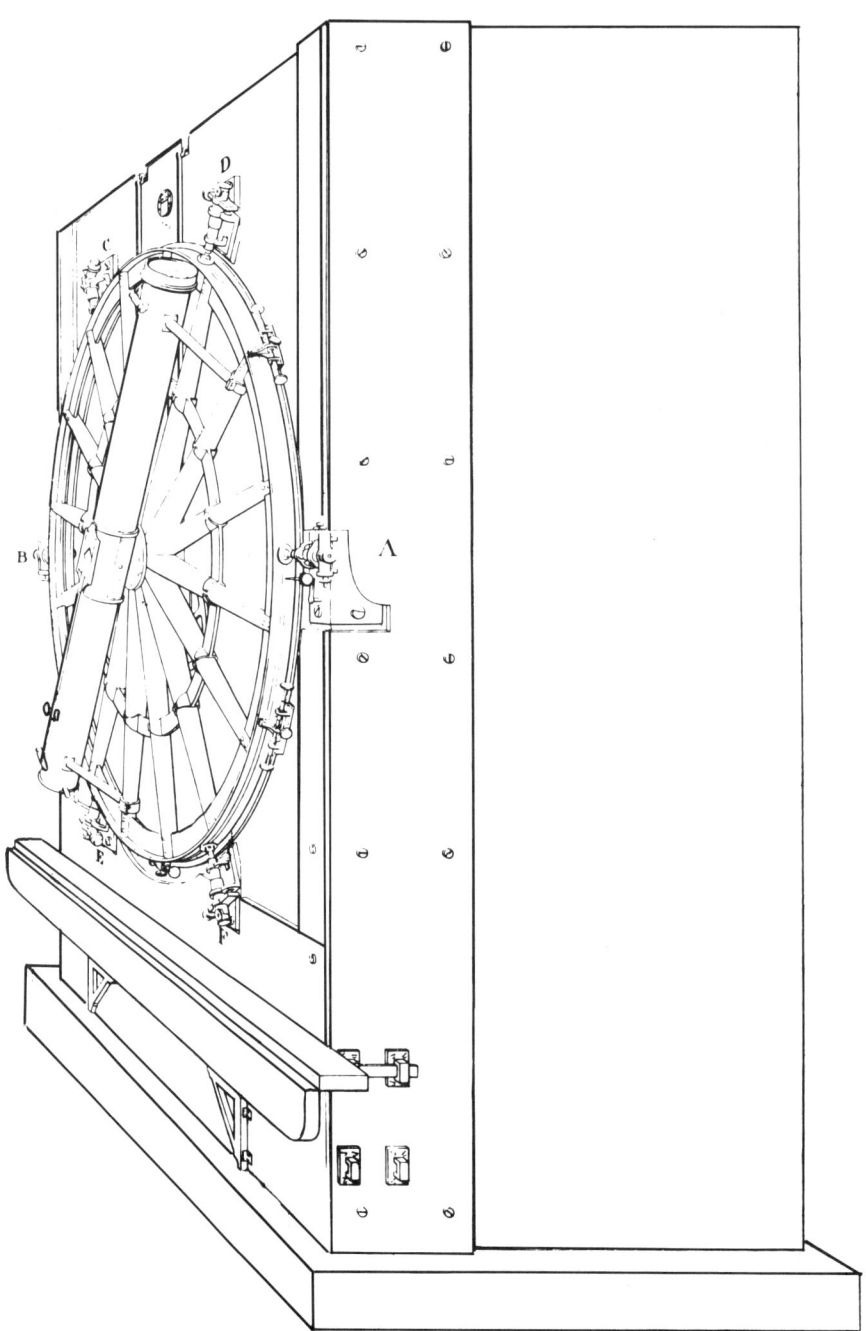

6 *Troughton's Mural Circle at Greenwich, a copy of which was sent to the Cape*

him the Gold Medal of the Royal Astronomical Society in 1835 and was Radcliffe Observer at Oxford, 1839-1859. He was the only astronomer, albeit inexperienced, to visit Fallows during the latter's life at the Cape; the two men became firm friends and Fallows continued to advise Johnson until his death, a debt acknowledged in the introduction to Johnson's catalogue.

With the instruments safely installed and working at the end of 1829, Fallows must have thought his troubles were at last over. He set to work with Dollond's large Transit and succeeded admirably with this instrument, which he never ceased to praise. The Mural Circle, (Figure 6) however, was altogether a different matter. This instrument, expensive and supposedly the equal of any in the world, would not perform satisfactorily. Consistent readings could not be obtained and only when Fallows took the average of the six microscopes around its graduated circle - a laborious task - could he get meaningful results. Despite extensive tests the cause of the trouble could not be found. The only possibility seemed to be damage caused by the fall in landing the Circle, but no damage was visible. The problem was very serious; a star catalogue could not be produced from transit observations alone, and to read all six microscopes slowed down observations to a crawl - and there would always be the dissatisfaction arising from not understanding the cause of the trouble. To return the Mural Circle to England for inspection would cause a further delay of at least six months. Fallows was despondent and saw the reputation that he had hoped to gain recede beyond his grasp.

Nevertheless, Fallows's ambitions drove him hard, and his observing books show that he observed on almost every clear night in 1829 and 1830, with interruptions only for sporadic illnesses. Problems continued to appear; because Fallows was unable to provide fuel "to enable them to Cook and dry their wet Clothing after exposure to the Rain" the military guard were withdrawn on 1 July 1829. In reporting this, Fallows complained that "on the same night a considerable quantity of Timber with the Kings Mark as well as some of my own property was stolen... were the building inclosed by a wall or some other means so as to secure the safety of the Instruments at night in particular from missile weapons thrown through the Chases (which must be open in a fine night) the sense of security would relieve the observers from any unpleasant feelings".

In September 1829 the two domes at last arrived from England and were installed under Skirrow's supervision, being completed on 24 December. They were made of copper and brass, 14 feet in diameter, rotatable and with a shuttered opening, and cost £3 000. One of the instruments intended to be erected under a dome was a 14-feet reflector made by Sir William Herschel for the Glasgow Observatory, and sold by them to the Board of Longitude for use at the Cape. Fallows never had an opportunity to unpack this instrument from its box.

Captain Ronald, who appears to have done very little to assist Fallows, became ill and took sick leave. He sailed for England on 18 October 1830.

8   The Royal Observatory, c.1830 (detail)

7
The Royal Observatory, c.1830,
by an unknown artist (detail)

Fallows, correctly suspecting that Ronald intended never to return, wrote to the Admiralty demanding that he either return or resign; his resignation arrived on 29 March 1831.

In anticipation of this event, Fallows looked for a clerk to assist in the copying of observations. In later years Piazzi Smyth reported that "The advertisement for a clerk having appeared, numbers of dashing gaudily dressed young men on horses applied; but at last, one poor thin unhealthy youth came hastely plodding on foot past the window: 'that's my man' Mr Fallows immediately exclaimed." The youth, James Robertson, engaged from 1 December 1830, remained at the Observatory until Ronald's replacement arrived.

In January and February 1829 Fallows erected meridian pillars for the adjustment of the Mural Circle and Transit Instrument. These substantial pillars supported a brass mechanism carrying a small dot on which the telescopes could be aligned. Two pillars were built to the north, near the junction of the Liesbeek and Salt rivers, and one to the south just outside the Observatory. The latter is still there, with Fallows's name inscribed on the cement top; the north meridian pillars were demolished or covered some years ago.

The Observatory just after its completion is depicted in two watercolours, Figures 7 and 8, by an unknown artist. Although undated, on the following grounds we may with some confidence ascribe them to the year 1830 or early 1831: The presence of the domes indicates a date later than December 1829; the absence of porches to the back doors (see Chapter 2) requires a date earlier than 1833. Fallows's successor was unmarried, so the couple seen in Figure 8 outside the Astronomer's residence (West Wing) are, in all probability, Fallows and his wife. We will shortly see that Fallows was too ill to emerge from his house subsequent to April 1831.

Before relating the sad end to the Fallows era, let us again review the brighter side of his life in Cape Town. Despite Fallows's labours at the Observatory, he was able to play a useful role in the cultural life of the town. It is to be remembered that, as a Fellow of the Royal Society, he was probably looked to as the most distinguished scientist in the Colony, and his presence was welcomed on many committees. His interests were catholic. He was on the committees of the South African Infirmary Fund (established in 1823), the Church of England Prayer Book and Tract Society (founded in 1824) and (as Chairman) the Committee for Managing the Affairs of the Intended English Church During its Erection (1829). On 5 August 1825 he became a committee member and on 29 February 1828 a Trustee of the South African Library (he resigned "for certain weighty reasons" on 13 August 1828). He and Andrew Smith led the attempt in 1825 to establish a South African Literary and Philosophical Society, which was squashed by Lord Charles Somerset. After Somerset's departure, the South African Institution (forerunner of the present Royal Society of South Africa) was established and on 27 June 1829 Fallows was made one of its first Vice Presidents. From 1827 to 1829 he served as Vice President of the short-lived Cape of Good Hope Horticultural Society; and he was an honorary member and most frequent attender of the Wine Committee, set up on 26 January 1826 to advise the Governor on methods of improving Cape Wines. Fallows was a Freemason at the Good Hope Lodge, and acted as Provincial Grand Chaplain at the laying of the foundation stone of St George's Church on 28 April 1830.

In October 1827 he received permission from the Lieutenant Governor to perform Divine Service in a room (the southern-most of the West Wing) of the Observatory. Each Sunday he held a service there for his friends. On 23 June 1830 the Senior Colonial Chaplain, the Revd George Hough, officiated at the Observatory in the marriage of one of Fallows's closest friends - the explorer, author and Cape Town merchant George Thompson. On 15 August of that year, Fallows baptized "William August, a Slave Boy" in his chapel.

Late in 1829 Fallows was able to send home his first observations with the Transit, amounting to some two thousand timings, and found that on the Mural Circle the average of six microscopes gave results consistent "to a degree of nicety which cheers up the observer and renders his work promising". From April to October 1830, however, "It pleased God to visit this observatory with severe sickness, first Bile, then Scarlet Fever... and for some weeks, I had to be carried in blankets every Sunday & wind up my Clocks".

After Capt Ronald left, Fallows had only his wife to assist him with the observations. She had had the distinction of discovering a comet in March of 1830; it was independently discovered by several other people. Mrs Fallows worked the Mural Circle, setting on the same star as her husband; as soon as he had finished with the Transit he rushed over to the Mural and

Immediately on hearing of Fallows's death, Commodore Schomberg put his Chaplain, the Reverend John Fry, in charge of the Observatory. Mrs Fallows sold her furniture and sailed for England in the Amity on 13 September taking with her all of her husband's papers and unpublished observations, which she sent to the Admiralty on arrival. The observations were eventually reduced by the Astronomer Royal, Sir George Airy, and published, together with an historical introduction, in the Memoirs of the Royal Astronomical Society in 1851. Airy thought very highly of the quality of Fallows's observations and there is no doubt that if Fallows had lived to complete his observations and publish a catalogue, he would have received all the recognition he desired.

It must be admitted that Fallows was not very capable of dealing with people nor experienced in organisation and a less naive person might have succeeded in progressing faster. Maclear said of him: "I have waded through Mr Fallows observations and records. That good man meant posterity to shift for itself. Even the year is but once or twice entered on the Cape Town observing sheets... In short, beyond his mathematical information he was a perfect child". A contemporary added "It is difficult to conceive a man of such simplicity of character and such absence of knowledge of the world in the nineteenth century"."

His success in constructing the Royal Observatory, despite conditions that would have defeated a less tenacious character, was notable but unsupported by the short time left to him to make his scientific reputation, as a result of which his name has fallen into obscurity. That his life was shortened as much by the effects of unhelpful and critical Governments and a recalcitrant Mural Circle, as by disease cannot be doubted, and he deserves a more prominent niche in history as a Martyr to Science.

Fallows is commemorated in only one place: the West Wing of the Royal Observatory has a brass plate informing the visitor that this, the Astronomer's residence, is called Fallows House. This follows the precedent set at the Royal Greenwich Observatory, where the residence is known as Flamsteed House, after the first Astronomer Royal.

read off the microscopes. In this way they kept going until 7 February 1831 on the Mural, and with a few isolated observations on the Transit until 30 March of that year. After this Fallows was too ill, with a recurrence of scarlet fever, to continue. That disease had been particularly virulent in Cape Town during 1830, and Fallows seems to have been re-infected with it in 1831.

On 8 April the senior officer at Simon's Town, Commodore C.M.Schomberg of HMS Maidstone, was obliged to write to the Admiralty to inform them that Fallows "has been under the necessity of desisting from his arduous duties, by illness, proceeding from over fatigue and unceasing application to his important employments... Mr Fallows has always complained of want of proper Assistants, and I am justified in stating, that had it not been for Mrs Fallows' efforts, some of his very important observations would have failed on different occasions". On 2 May, the Naval surgeons at Simon's Town issued a certificate stating that his scarlet fever had developed into dropsy and jaundice; they had performed an operation but any recovery was expected to be slow. Fallows returned to the Observatory but by 1 July he had concluded that he would only recover if he left the Cape, and accordingly advertised in the Gazette for his outstanding debts to be sent to the Observatory. On the 12th he made his will, George Thompson and John Skirrow acting as witnesses. On 25 July 1831 he died.

A correspondent described his funeral in a letter to the Commercial Advertiser on 1 August; from this eulogy we need only quote Fallows's description as an "honest, upright and single minded man", and the fact that his funeral was attended by "men of every rank, of every persuasion, almost of every shade of character", the latter comment probably resulting from the presence of Fayrer! Fallows was buried in front of the Observatory "sunk at his request, the depth of 12 feet". This great depth was common in Europe at the time - an era of bodysnatching, but one wonders why Fallows requested such treatment at the Cape where there were no Medical Schools. Mrs Fallows arranged for a slab of Robben Island stone to cover her husband's grave. On this his age is stated to have been 43 years, whereas he was actually in his fortythird year; the same error appears on the memorial stone that Mrs Fallows installed in the All Saints' Churchyard at Cockermouth after her return to England.

A short biography appeared in the Literary Gazette for 1 December 1832, from which only the following footnote is remarkable: "...the Colonial Government of 1827 did, by its series of petty meannesses, greatly annoy and injure the mind and body of the Astronomer Royal". This is the only indication we have that Fallows found difficulties with the Lieutenant Governor, Sir Richard Bourke; any disputes between them evidently healed, because Fallows's name is inscribed, as one of the subscribers, on a Cape Silver Tray, presented to Bourke on his retirement, which is currently in the Africana Museum.

2 Thomas Henderson
1831-1833

On reception of Captain Ronald's resignation, the Admiralty had appointed Lieutenant William Meadows, R.N., to the position of Assistant. Hearing of Fallows's serious illness, they hastened Meadows's departure and he embarked in the Zenobia at Portsmouth on 22 August 1831 - before the news of Fallows's death had arrived. Meadows, his wife and a servant arrived in Table Bay on 4 November to be confronted with the sad news - and the disturbing discovery that their lodgings in the East Wing were occupied by the Reverend John Fry and his wife, the latter of whom suffered from leprosy. When he insisted that the interior of the East Wing should be completely cleaned and repainted before he would be willing to occupy it, Meadows was initiated immediately into the difficulties of persuading the Naval Officer, J.Deas Thompson, at Simon's Town to expend money on anything without explicit authority from the Admiralty.

In their search for a successor to Fallows, the Admiralty faced a dearth of suitably orientated Cambridge mathematicians. A possibility might have been George Biddell Airy, Senior Wrangler in 1823, but he already had ambitions of attaining the position of Astronomer Royal at Greenwich. The search therefore widened to include observatory assistants and prominent amateurs. Of these, two people were considered the most eligible; William Richardson and Thomas Henderson. Richardson was Fourth Assistant at Greenwich and an experienced practical astronomer. Henderson was an amateur. As the Naval Hydrographer pointed out, "...the chief points of difference are that Mr R. was originally a blacksmith, and Mr. H. had a competent education; - and that the latter is single, while the former has a wife and family". Education and bachelorhood won: it was as well, for Richardson was later involved in a scandal.

Thomas Henderson (Figure 9) was born in Dundee on 28 December 1798. Educated at grammar school and the Dundee Academy, destined for the law profession, he excelled in every subject. At the age of fifteen he was apprenticed to a solicitor; in his leisure time he began to study astronomy. In 1819 he moved to Edinburgh to complete his legal studies in an office of law. There his talents were immediately noticed and he was appointed Advocate's Clerk to Lord Eldvin. He later succeeded to the position of secretary to the Lord Advocate. During these professional employments he came into contact with astronomers at the University of Edinburgh, who encouraged his interests in astronomy and allowed him to use the small observatory on Calton Hill. From 1824 onwards, Henderson published a number of important papers, mostly of a computational nature. These and his careful observations at Calton Hill would have done credit to a full-time professional astronomer, and he almost captured a Professorship at Edinburgh and the Superintendency of the Nautical Almanac. By 1831 he was well qualified for a senior position in British astronomy, and the Admiralty offered him the Cape post.

Henderson had a weak constitution and an eye condition that at times made him nearly blind - although this never seems to have interfered with his observations (of bright stars). The reports of the health hazards at the Cape and Henderson's reluctance to leave Scotland, inclined him to refuse the Cape position, but his friends persuaded him to accept it in the expectation that it would best further his interests. He reluctantly accepted and was appointed on 15 October 1831. He sailed from Spithead in the Melville on 22 January 1832 and arrived at Simon's Town on 22 March, taking up residence at the Observatory on 8 April.

Henderson's short stay at the Cape was one of intense industry. He quickly confirmed that the Mural Circle gave satisfactory results if all the microscopes were read at each observation. Lieutenant Meadows, using the Transit Instrument, was inspired by Henderson's zeal and between them they made nearly ten thousand measurements of star positions during the year. These constituted the first large body of accurate fundamental positions in the southern hemisphere.

Early in 1833 Henderson started a new time service. The Observatory cash book for 4 January 1833 records "To John Constable for castings... and for a brass barrel percussion pistol for the making of night signals to vessels in Table Bay, for the regulation of their chronometers, £5 5s". With this gun and a pocket chronometer, Henderson each night climbed on to the roof of the Observatory and fired a charge of black powder at an advertised time. The flash was bright enough for any sailor to see (if his telescope was correctly aimed). The brass pistol, and its powder flask, are now in the South African Museum.

Observational duties left little time for other work, and it appears that Henderson played no part in the intellectual life of Cape Town. He attempted to improve the amenities at the Observatory by entreaties to Admiral Frederic Warren at Simon's Town and Captain Beaufort in England. Admiral Warren only allowed "the immediate erection of the Porches and two Privies to be built, which is all that I conceive to be absolutely necessary". On 1 January 1833 John Skirrow wrote to Henderson to state that he had been authorised to attend to these additions, but Henderson objected to the plans and promptly wrote to Warren "on the subject of the conveniences in a deliberate but manly tone", declining these but requesting that the porches be erected. Despite many letters of complaint, Skirrow was slow to act,

9   *Thomas Henderson*

and this coming on top of his other problems so frustrated Henderson that in a fit of anger he decided to resign his appointment and return to England. His decision was made at the end of April 1833; on the 27 of that month he wrote letters to Herschel and to his friend (and successor) Thomas Maclear to tell them of his decision. To Maclear he wrote "It would give me much pleasure and perhaps contribute to the recovery of my health and spirits, were I to have once more the gratification of seeing yourself, Mrs Maclear and family around your own fireside... I would then tell Mrs M. and Miss Mary Maclear all about my residence in Dismal Swamp among Slaves and Savages...plenty of insidious venomous deadly snakes. No one sets down a foot on the grounds of the Royal Observatory in the warm season, till he is certain that he is not treading upon a Snake in the grass. What would you think if on putting out your Candle to step into bed, you were to find one lurking beside the Bed?"

"Dismal Swamp" was an epithet that Henderson frequently applied to the Observatory. Surrounded on each side by rivers, which often overflowed in winter, forming stagnant marshland, the Observatory was plagued by mosquitoes and not conducive to good health. However, the locality and the difficulties of obtaining workmen were not the only frustrations. There were also the Meadows: after Maclear had been at the Cape for some months, he wrote to Henderson "Those into whose hands you as a single man fell are without doubt the most melancholic, discontented croaking helpless couple I ever met with... What then must be the consequence of your breathing daily and hourly the atmosphere of discontent and to have it instilled into your ear that the government of your country cared but little for the result of your labours".

An example of the Meadows's feelings is given in the poem that Mrs Meadows in 1832 sent to friends in England:

Description of the Royal Observatory, Cape of Good Hope"

Should I call on my pen to describe in detail
The aspect around us, its efforts would fail
Since the task is so hard a just picture to make
When a negative scene for our subject we take -
We mix not in the stir of a city or town
For to us their allurements or cares are unknown,
Nor live we where nature exhibits her store
But to wed us to rural attractions the more
Nor move we on Ocean with proud sail unfurled,
To gain knowledge or wealth from the old or new world.
No, it is not like land and it is not like sea
But lest it be asked, where this strange home can be?
'Tis as well to confess that it stands on a plain
Over which the eye wanders for beauty in vain
No tree lends its foliage, -no warbler is heard

10   View of the Observatory from the Flats, May 1833, by Charles D'Oyly (detail)

>For green are the haunts of the sweet singing bird;
>The owl screams by night round the pond'rous Pile
>And the terrified frogs cease their croaking the while
>Dread serpents dispute our just claims to a place
>Which ages ago was assigned to their race.
>And they lurk in our pathway, our chambers molest
>Old Eolus for pastime delights to whirl round
>The vanes of ten mills which are seen from Snake Mound.
>The "Slough of Despond" intercepts our main road,
>And near "Dismal Swamp" stands our stately abode.

Taken together with his earlier reluctance to leave Scotland, Henderson's resignation is hardly surprising. It was nevertheless a courageous act, for he had only a pension of £100 per annum (from his service to the Lord Advocate) on which to subsist. In a letter to the Admiralty on 27 May he resigned his position, left the Observatory in the charge of Lieutenant Meadows, and together with his official letter of resignation sailed to England in the Zenobia on the following day.

By good fortune, one of the Cape's best artists, Sir Charles D'Oyly, portrayed the Observatory in the same month that Henderson decamped. Figure 10, penned on 17 May 1833, shows that the porches over the northern doors of the main building had been completed. Further to the north is a small cluster of buildings discussed more fully in the next Chapter. To the north-east (right foreground) is the stable built by Captain Ronald. To the south of the Observatory are the Transit meridian pillar, a low edifice which is probably the fence around Fallows's grave (see later, Figure 14) and a flagpole. Beyond the flagpole is an unidentified building.

On 14 June, during its voyage to England, the Zenobia called at St Helena and Henderson paid a surprise visit to Manuel Johnson. Johnson had recently noted that the star Alpha Centauri has a large space motion, is therefore a nearby star and a prime candidate for measurement of parallax (an astronomical term related to the distance of a star). He had written to Henderson with this information shortly before the latter abandoned the Cape. Fortuitously, Henderson had made a large number of observations of Alpha Centauri and proceeded, on his return to Scotland, to analyse his results. His conclusion was unequivocal: the star had a parallax large enough to be determined even with the rebellious Mural Circle. Thus was the first stellar parallax measured. However, independently and concurrently, F.W.Struve in Russia and W.Bessel in Germany each measured the parallax of a star in the northern hemisphere. Their results were announced first, but to Henderson must be awarded the credit for being the first to make observations from which a parallax could be extracted. This must be tempered by the fact that Henderson's achievement was largely serendipitous - he did not actually set out to measure a parallax. The Royal Observatory, however, received international recognition for the first time.

On 1 October 1834 Henderson was appointed to the positions of (the first) Astronomer Royal for Scotland, Professor of Astronomy at the University of Edinburgh and Director of the Calton Hill Observatory. He resided in his beloved Edinburgh, working up his Cape observations and continuing to observe, until his early death on 23 November 1844. Like Fallows before him, he failed to complete the reductions or publish the bulk of his many observations of star positions.

3   Thomas Maclear
    1833-1870

The receipt in England of Henderson's letters of April 1833 forewarned the Admiralty of his intention to resign. Once again they had to cast around for a qualified astronomer for the Cape. There was still no professional, versed in the science of meridian astronomy, suitable or willing to serve. However, the reputation of another amateur (considered but passed over at the time of Henderson's appointment) had in the meantime flourished to an extent that the Admiralty could no longer ignore his claims. Early in June 1833 they offered the succession to Thomas Maclear.

Maclear (Figure 11) was born at Newtown Stewart, County Tyrone, Ireland, on 17 March 1794. An early proficiency in Latin led to young Thomas being groomed for the Church. His objections to this intended life led to a permanent breach with his father and, at the age of fifteen, he was sent to England to be cared for by his maternal uncles, Sir George and Dr T. Magrath, both of whom were eminent surgeons. The latter had a private practice in Biggleswade, Bedfordshire, and to him the young Maclear was apprenticed in May 1808.
  In 1814 Maclear took up residence in London to study at Guy's and St Thomas Hospitals - in surgery he was instructed by the famous Sir Astley Cooper. The following year he achieved great success in his examinations and was elected a Member of the Royal College of Surgeons. His appointment as House Surgeon to the Bedford Infirmary returned him to the vicinity of his uncle, with whom he entered into partnership in 1823. Two years later he married Mary, daughter of Theed Pearse of Bedford, and they settled in Biggleswade.
  During the 1820's Maclear became increasingly enamoured of astronomy, spending much of his spare time in learning mathematical methods and observing with a small telescope. He became very active in astronomical circles, attending meetings in London and lectures given around the country; indeed, he met his future wife at a lecture on astronomy. In these pursuits he was encouraged by Theed Pearse, who had an amateur interest in astronomy, and also by one of the most colourful characters of the nineteenth century, William Henry Smyth.
  Captain Smyth had served in the navy since he was a boy. He saw action against Napoleon's fleet, and later acted as an hydrographer to chart the Mediterranean. While there, he took an antiquarian interest in Italian arti-

11   Thomas Maclear

facts, collected coins and married the daughter of the British Consul in Naples. Two sons were born to them in Naples, the second of whom, Charles Piazzi, was named after Guiseppe Piazzi, notable Italian astronomer and a close friend of Smyth.

Captain Smyth retired to Bedford in 1828 (rising eventually to Admiral on the retired list) and built himself a substantial observatory - the principal telescope of which is now in the Science Museum at South Kensington. He became a very active amateur astronomer, specializing in measurements of double stars.

Maclear was a frequent visitor to the Smyth household, where he met many of Smyth's distinguished acquaintances, of whom Sir Francis Beaufort (Hydrographer, and inventor of the well-known scale of wind forces) and Sir John Herschel were to become lifelong friends. The stimulus that Maclear thus received led him to build his own observatory at Biggleswade, equipped with a small transit instrument and a telescope borrowed from the Royal Astronomical Society. The results that he obtained with these telescopes, and the calculations that he performed - some of them in collaboration with Thomas Henderson - led to the rise in his reputation amongst British astronomers, so much so that in December 1831 he was elected to that most august of scientific bodies, the Royal Society.

Maclear did not immediately accept the Admiralty's offer of the Cape position, which had been made largely at the suggestion of Beaufort. His salary in Biggleswade amounted to about £800 per annum, whereas his Cape income would be only £600. Maclear's uncle, expecting a brilliant career for him in medicine, opposed the move and refused to assist him financially in his travel. Furthermore, Henderson had written to tell him of conditions at Dismal Swamp and from a friend he received a copy of Mrs Meadows's poem. For Maclear, however, the hobby of astronomy had become more exciting than his profession and, with the support of his wife, and the intention of residing at the Cape for only seven years, he decided to accept the position and risk the consequences. Not all caution was thrown to the wind: suspecting that Henderson's account might be distorted, he wrote to Mrs Fallows for a description of life at the Observatory and received a satisfactory answer. He also had reason to believe that his first few years at the Cape would be particularly exciting and to some extent buttressed by a strong ally, for he knew that Sir John Herschel was about to embark for the Cape.

John Frederick William Herschel was born at Slough on 7 March 1792, the only child of one of history's most famous astronomers, Sir William Herschel. Unlike his father, who was raised as a musician but with little formal education, John's early personal tuition was followed by attendance at Eton. He then entered St John's College, Cambridge and graduated as Senior Wrangler in 1813. In the same year, at the remarkably early age of twenty-one, and in recognition of his outstanding mathematical abilities, he was elected a Fellow of the Royal Society. For the next few years he vacillated between the Church (his father's choice), law, optics, mathematics, and chemical experiments. In 1816 Sir William, then seventy-eight years old, sought his son's assistance in continuing astronomical observations at Slough, as a result of which John abandoned Cambridge and turned his attention to practical astronomy. Over the next fifteen years he repeated his father's survey of the northern sky, finding many previously unrecorded nebulae and double stars.

The expediency of extending the survey to the southern hemisphere must frequently have crossed Herschel's mind. In 1830 an event occurred which precipitated a decision. Davies Gilbert, who had been President of the Royal Society for three years, announced his intention of resigning at the end of the year. A group of Fellows proposed the Duke of Sussex as candidate for Presidency. The Duke had become a Fellow principally by virtue of his royal connections, so the proposition angered the scientists in the Society and they determined to contest the election with a candidate of their own. Their choice of Herschel, who acceded with reluctance, is a clear indication of his pre-eminent standing in contemporary science. At the election Herschel lost by 111 votes to 119. The controversy and bad-feeling generated during the process of election canvassing was distasteful to Herschel. A few weeks later he was planning to leave the country: on 9 January 1831 he wrote to Fallows at the Cape "Now shall I tell you a scheme I have in view. It is one which will finally depend on contingencies, as I am now a family man and have one child already and a prospect of more, am not quite my own member, I am likewise fettered by domestic considerations, can at present only speculate on the future. But I have a great notion of packing up my 20 feet reflector and coming and passing a year or two at the Cape, to pick up some nebulae in the South and for a peep at the Magellanic Clouds". Fallows was too ill to answer this letter.

"Domestic considerations" probably referred to Herschel's mother, whom he was reluctant to leave. Even though her death in January 1832 released Herschel from that obligation, preparations for the trip, and completion of his northern hemisphere work, took more time than he expected. Not until November 1833 was everything prepared and on the 13th of that month Herschel, accompanied by his wife, three children, a servant, an assistant and numerous boxes containing the 20-feet telescope, embarked on the Mountstuart Elphinstone, 611 tons, for the Cape. Fellow passengers were the newly appointed Governor of the Cape, Sir Benjamin D'Urban, and his wife.

Maclear hoped to accompany the Herschels on the Mountstuart Elphinstone, but, finding the cost of passage too great (£400 for himself and his entourage - the Government gave him only £50 towards his travel costs) he had to settle for a navy ship, the Tam O'Shanter. Maclear, his wife and five daughters, a governess, a nursemaid, Thomas Bowler (Maclear's manservant), and their best furniture embarked on 10 October 1833. The journey was long, rough and extremely unpleasant. Only five days out, anchored in The Downs waiting for an unfavourable gale to desist, Maclear wrote to Herschel "This vessel is in a most filthy state. How I repent my caution in money matters. Although a poor man I would this moment (were the flight possible) give Heathorn [the shipping agent] his £400. I always intended to spend £100 for the purpose of being in the same vessel with you...".

The diary that Maclear kept on the voyage shows that his services as a medical man were frequently required to ease the distress in his family. He made position determinations whenever the weather would allow - initially from interest, but later from expediency as the Captain was "too fond of the brandy bottle". The phosphoresence in the wake of the ship also interested him; he found on examination under his microscope that the particles responsible "proved to be animalculae".

The Maclears arrived at the Cape "heartily sick of our sea trip" on 7 January 1834. Writing to Dr John Lee (originally Fiot), another Bedford amateur astronomer, he reported "When I landed on Sunday morning I hired a gig and drove to the observatory, where - feasting my eyes (and finding that I could make a favourable report to Mrs Maclear) I remained about half an hour, returned to the ship and landed my family... my youngest child was taken suddenly ill on Tuesday and died on Thursday. A sad blow to our spirits on landing at the Cape". No more encouraging was Lieutenant Meadows's greeting to Maclear: "So Sir, you have determined to accept this wretched appointment". But Maclear recognised the potential of the Observatory and was able to give Herschel an enthusiastic account of it when the Mountstuart Elphinstone arrived in Table Bay on 16 January. To Dr Lee he wrote "The observatory... is a beautiful building, substantial and well situated. A clear view except at one point to the S.W., where Table Mountain and the Lions' Rump cut off a few degrees. The panoramic views Bowler took, stationed a few feet in front of the observatory will at once convey an idea of the surrounding scenery... The Transit room is well contrived. The shutters open by Pulleys in small lengths of three feet at a time. This is a great advantage where high winds prevail. The Circle room is provided in the same way. On the whole the Transit and Circle rooms are better arranged and constructed, than any I have seen or read of. The domes are badly placed and at present useless, because the shutters cannot be opened. ...Sir J. and Lady Herschel were much pleased with the observatory, and agree with me in opinion that the spot is well chosen for the purpose. It is certainly not convenient for us who reside in it, and merely from this cause, that no steps whatsoever have been taken to make a road to it, the consequence is, that about 50 or £100 per annum additional expense is entailed upon me, in keeping a servant and cart more than I otherwise should require, and there is in reality no stabling or offices of any sort, or Inclosure to the building".

Thomas Bowler, referred to in Maclear's letter, was the son of a former

13   Bowler pencil sketch, c.1834, looking south-west (detail)

14   Bowler pencil sketch, c.1834, looking north-west (detail)

12 *Cluster of huts in the grounds of the Royal Observatory, by Thomas Bowler*

housekeeper to Dr Lee. Recommended by Lee, Bowler was paid out of Maclear's own pocket to act as a footman and to learn astronomical computations. In July 1834 Maclear fired the dissolute Fayrer, who was still drawing the annual salary of £100 allowed him by Fallows, and appointed Bowler in his place. After a year his progress and conduct (which had included insolence to Mrs Maclear) proved unsatisfactory and he too was dismissed. Maclear explained to Lee that "He should not have been at the observatory till this time but for a sense of gratitude to you" and "He informs me that he has got a situation in a gentlemans family to teach the children 'drawing and the use of Globes etc.'". Bowler went on to become one of the most important artists in the history of the Cape Colony, pictorially documenting many historic events in Cape life. To him we are indebted for some twenty or so pictures of the Royal Observatory, the first of which, the Panorama referred to in Maclear's letter, is still at the Observatory. Bowler's earliest known attempt at a watercolour shows (Figure 12) a group of buildings in the grounds of the Observatory. He realised the significance of this group; the middle section is the 1820 Settlers' hut used by Fallows as his temporary observatory.

After settling in, Maclear had an interview with Admiral Warren, who was evidently relieved to find that Maclear's attitude was very different from that of Henderson, and who promised to support him in improving the facilities at the Observatory. As a result, Maclear applied to the Admiralty for £1000 to construct outhouses and a boundary fence. While he awaited a reply, work was at last started on the water-closets. By the middle of April 1834 these, and two meridian pillars about a quarter of a mile south of the Observatory, were completed. The Observatory at this time is well-depicted in Bowler's two undated pencil sketches (Figures 13 and 14). To the south of the main building were the Transit meridian pillar, a flagpole, and a wooden picket fence erected to prevent cattle from desecrating Fallows's grave. On the north side, one of the notorious water-closets is seen appended to the inner side of the West Wing. To the right of the main building, i.e. to the west of it, is the group of huts shown in more detail in Figure 12.

At the same time that the Maclears were settling into their new profession and residence, the Herschels were making their home at Feldhausen, an estate at Claremont which Herschel at first rented and later purchased. Herschel's choice of the Wynberg area was strongly influenced by Henderson. Not having received a reply to his 1831 letter to Fallows, Herschel had written on 14 December 1832 to Henderson at the Cape to make enquiries about observing conditions and suitable sites. Henderson replied "As to the residence, the County about Wynberg I believe (and it seems to be the universal opinion) is the best in the Cape district... It is not so much sheltered from the gales as is desirable; but I know no place in any part of the Cape

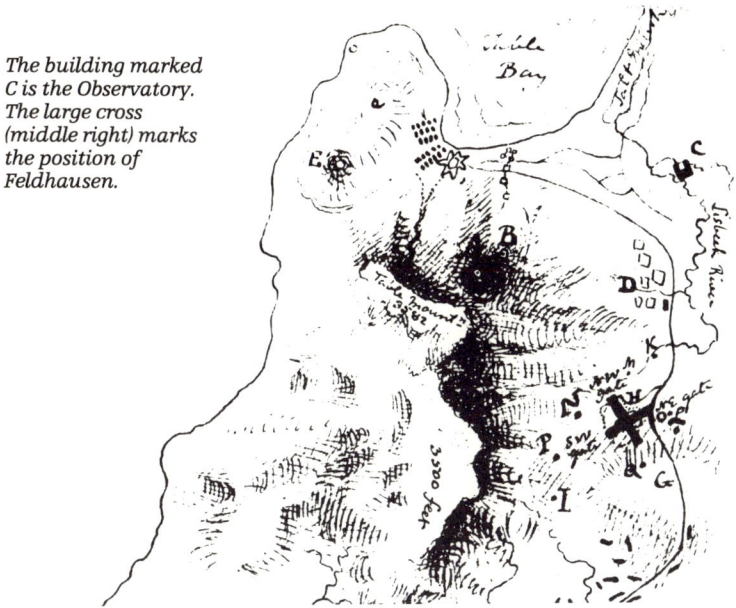

The building marked C is the Observatory. The large cross (middle right) marks the position of Feldhausen.

15   Map of the Cape Peninsula by Sir John Herschel (detail)

Peninsula that is sheltered; and I understand that Wynberg is as little exposed as any place - certainly far less so than the observatory, which I believe to be on the most exposed spot in the Country".

In only fifteen working days, Herschel erected his great telescope in an orchard "half a pistol shot" from the house, and started on his survey of the southern heavens: a task that was to take him four years.

The relative situations of Feldhausen and the Observatory are shown in Herschel's sketch map of the Peninsula (Figure 15). Although only four miles separated them, bad roads and bustling activity served, except for occasional visits, to keep the astronomers apart. They did, however, maintain communications by means of letters conveyed by their servants (and also via the general tradesmen), writing at times twice daily. A large part of their initial correspondence concerned the Mural Circle.

The troublesome Mural Circle received Maclear's early attention; if he was to make effective use of this instrument it would be advisable first to try to correct its deficiencies. His first approach was to read the microscopes at every circle division; a note to Dr Lee remarks that "There will be about 15 000 revolutions of Microscope made in this undertaking. I close the window shutters in the day and read off day and night by lamp light, while Bowler enters the results in a Book". This intensive effort lasted from 1 to 17 March, after which Maclear was able to confirm the assertions of both

Fallows and Henderson that the average of all six microscopes could be relied on. The value of having Herschel near at hand now appeared - he suggested a method using "levers of contact" whereby small errors in the pivot of the instrument could be magnified and easily measured. Despite all their efforts, the cause of the irregularities defied analysis and Maclear was compelled to continue with the instrument in the same laborious manner as his predecessors.

The Admiralty's response to Maclear's request for building funds amounted to only £500, a paltry amount when it is remembered that £10 000 had been cut from the original plans. Maclear found it necessary to supplement the grant with money from his own pocket: on 4 February 1835 he wrote to Airy "With respect to domestic affairs, the appearance of this place is considerably improved, and some essential comforts have been secured. But my expenses in these operations have been formidable, I cannot longer continue them. About £100 have been spent in clearing of weeds, rubbish and divers operations in planting seeds &c. & 28£ in putting down an Iron pump. The latter will I have no doubt be refunded by the Government. The former there is little chance of. I consider it sunk or a subscription towards making the place decent... A man of the name of Tate who assisted Mr Fallows in fixing the Instruments & who performed the fine Carpentry of the Dwelling house, has given me a history of the place, from which I gather that someone must have imposed upon Henderson by magnifying the dangers from Reptiles &c, the truth of which he cannot have enquired into or troubled himself about... The principal annoyance I receive is from cattle, & persons riding by near the house. About two months back I gave a public notice that all cattle found on the observatory hill would be sent to the Pound, & I warned persons against committing any trespass. I have carried the threat into effect. About sixty head of cattle have been in prison. I dare say the Dutch could see the little 'English man' at old Nic. Without this display of resolution I could not keep the doors in better trim from filth than a Hottentot craal. Conceive a building as imposing & as well executed as the Cambridge observatory, surrounded by cows enjoying its shade ready to thrust their horns through the windows and a black fellow on the ground at a distance fast asleep & you have the picture this would present if submitted to".

The Admiralty grant enabled Maclear to construct the first permanent out-buildings and a boundary barrier. The latter was composed partly of a fence but the remainder had to be limited to a trench over one thousand yards long which, as Maclear explained in a letter to the astronomer Francis Baily was "5 feet wide at the top - four feet deep and three feet wide at the bottom; the soil and stones throw up, on which will be planted the prickly Pear (cactus) and the spike leafed Aloe. A most formidable barrier, requiring little or no repair, and permanent, since a great part of this trench is cut through stone, some solid, some loose. The stones thus dug up, go towards building the stable and its surrounding wall... The sensation of an inclosure is so in-

16   Camera Lucida drawing by Sir John Herschel, January 1837 (detail)

teresting - so new - that I absolutely wallow in the luxury, while with my hands in my pockets I look with pride at Bullock Waggons - Hottentots and idle trespassers being obliged to keep their distance".

The "stable" in fact consisted of a northward extention of the West Wing, forming a courtyard bounded on its west and north sides by buildings. These comprised a scullery, kitchen, stable and cart-house, with a loft over the latter in which the groom slept. The whole group formed an harmonious extension to the main building and was completed early in 1836.

Another modification to the general appearance of the Observatory was Maclear's addition of a Time Ball. In May 1834 Admiral Warren retired from Simonstown and was replaced at the end of the year by Admiral Patrick Campbell. Campbell's flag captain (and brother-in-law) Captain Robert Wauchope, was the inventor of the Time Ball, a device in which a ball was dropped at an advertised time in order that ships in harbour (or the general public) could determine the error and rate of their chronometers. Wauchope's proposal was taken up by James Pond and he erected a Time Ball at the Royal Greenwich Observatory in 1833. Campbell and Wauchope evidently persuaded Maclear that such an addition would be an improvement over the method he used - that of noting and publishing the time of the flash of the 9 p.m. cannon on Signal Hill - for shortly after their arrival Maclear was investigating its practicability. The refusal of the Colonial Government to pay for the Time Ball delayed its construction, and it was only on 30 September 1836 that Maclear was able to announce in the Government Gazette that the Time Ball had been erected to the southeast of the Observatory - it had replaced the flagpole previously sited there.

Herschel's camera lucida sketch (Figure 16) made on 2 January 1837 from about the position of Klerk's Kraal across the swamps of the Salt River, de-

17 Self-portrait of Charles Piazzi Smyth

picts the changed appearance of the Observatory. Along with the stables and Time Ball, an additional wooden workshop with thatched roof had been constructed, seen to the right of the Assistant's (originally Captain Ronald's) stable. Although many small shrubs and seeds of fir trees had been contributed by Herschel, the site was still barren of large trees.

From their first meeting, the personality of Lieutenant Meadows had irked Maclear, but the event that led to Meadows's resignation gave him far greater cause for censure. Insolent conduct on the part of "the profligate woman Lee in Mr Meadows service" led Maclear to insist on her removal from the premises. Meadows protested and in an interview with Maclear threatened to resign. Despite Maclear's warning of "the probable opinion of the world if he preferred leaving his situation to parting with that woman", Meadows applied for three months leave, with implications of never returning. The ménage à trois embarked on the Georgina for England on 25 December 1834, leaving Maclear "much moved to see reasoning beings leave a place because a designing female servant should have her way".

Fayrer - Scully - Ronald - Bowler - Meadows: The Observatory was ill-served by its Assistants, and Maclear was understandably anxious to secure a person who would be as industrious as himself and a credit to the Observatory. Fate - or rather parental influence - was to provide an unexpected and unorthodox but satisfactory answer.

In Bedford, Captain Smyth had been raising his children in an atmosphere of natural philosophy, art and astronomy. Young Charles Piazzi Smyth had shown an early talent for art and a predilection towards astronomy. Maclear's call for a sterling assistant came just as Piazzi was completing his schooling, and the Captain considered him to be a worthy candidate. Such was the Captain's influence in affairs astronomical, that on 9 October 1835 the sixteen year old Piazzi found himself disembarking from the Eagle to take up duties as First Assistant at the Royal Observatory. As Henderson wrote to Maclear: "it is not everyone who on leaving school has a post of £250 per annum conferred upon him. This was neither your luck nor mine".

Piazzi Smyth (Figure 17) had inherited from his father a robust physique, great stamina, a natural inquisitiveness and some eccentricities. The first two of these were undeniable assets: Maclear was a martinet, admitting in a letter to Airy that he had been working Piazzi eighteen hours a day. But Maclear's affection for the old Captain, and his memories of Piazzi at Bedford, led him to treat the boy "as one of my own", giving him at first board and lodging with the Maclear family. Herschel had also met Piazzi during visits to Bedford and was equally delighted to see him at the Cape, inviting him to "tea and stars" and on occasion feeling obliged to apologise to Maclear for having detained his Assistant for so long.

While at the Cape, Piazzi made extensive use of his talents as an artist. One of his early sketches is shown in the Frontispiece of this book.

Under Maclear's guidance, Piazzi Smyth soon became skilled in the use

The Apparatus employed in the Measurement of the Base I - the East end of the Base, & the Method of Boning

18   Drawing by C.P. Smyth (detail)

of the Mural Circle and, with Maclear at the Transit, meridian work continued apace. But then came an intrusion into the normal work of the Observatory, the start of a campaign that was to occupy Maclear for much of his thirty-six years service.

In 1751-3 the Abbé Nicolas Louis de la Caille (nowadays usually "Lacaille") visited the Cape in order to prepare a catalogue of the southern stars and also to measure an arc of meridian in the southern hemisphere. The latter task comprises an accurate survey of the distance between two points chosen to lie along a meridian (i.e. on a north-south line), together with accurate determination of the latitudes of the two points. The difference in latitude of the two ends, combined with the distance between them, yields a measurement of the Earth's radius. Lacaille's measured arc of meridian, lying between his observatory in Strand Street and a site at Klipfontein, gave an Earth radius significantly different from that measured at a similar latitude in the northern hemisphere, apparently demonstrating that the Earth is pear-shaped.

Despite the excellence of Lacaille's work, contemporary opinion was sceptical of his result. Over the years, recommendations to verify the result were made, the most insistent of which was that by Colonel George Everest, the famous surveyor who visited the Cape on his way to India in 1820 and who suspected that the reason for Lacaille's discrepant result lay in the gravitational attraction of Table Mountain. Everest met Fearon Fallows, who was impressed by the surveyor's argument and wrote to both Herschel and the Admiralty requesting permission to pursue the subject. The Admiralty were unsympathe-

(Cape of Good Hope 1837); together with a view of the Meridian Marks, the Line through the Air. In the Distance appears the ...VATORY.

tic at that time, but when Maclear arrived at the Cape one of his instructions was "to collect gradually information as to the most eligible place for the measurement of a base, and for the other geodesical operations, as well as on the local facilities and general practicability of such an undertaking".

A thorough search of the Government archives enabled Maclear to locate the exact position of Lacaille's observatory in Cape Town. In January 1836, as a trial trek, and also to avoid embroilment in a political issue menacing Cape Town, Maclear and Herschel went on a short expedition to Paarl. Satisfied with the results of these exercises, Maclear obtained permission from the Admiralty to re-survey Lacaille's arc of meridian.

In a preamble to the principal expedition, Maclear gained experience in survey work by laying out some trial baselines. He was then able to measure distances and heights of objects around Cape Town by triangulation from the extremities of these bases. His first endeavour was to measure a baseline on the Grand Parade, which he accomplished with a surveyor's chain on 26 November 1836. The correct procedure, however, was to employ measuring rods, supported on tressles, that could be compared with a standard rod brought out from England. With these in hand, Maclear laid off a baseline, one end of which was located at the north meridian mark of the Transit Instrument and the other at an unserviceable cannon sunk into the ground. Piazzi Smyth's delightful and informative sketch (Figure 18) shows the apparatus required for the work. Maclear is sitting at a theodolite as the "boning rods" are set in a straight line. The Observatory is seen in the background.

The actual measurement of the length of the baseline is depicted in another

19   Modus Operandi, by C.P. Smyth (detail)

of Piazzi's sketches (Figure 19). From Maclear's diary we learn that the individuals illustrated are, from left to right, Maclear, "a common labourer Klaas", Joseph Gibbs (the Observatory carpenter), "an engineer soldier", Lieutenant Williams, R.E., and Piazzi Smyth himself. The sketch is subtitled "a caricature" probably because Smyth, borrowing without shame from Michaelangelo, is depicted "creating the baseline". During the first attempt, in June 1837, wind blew two of the rods from their tressles and work had to be abandoned. Another, successful, attempt was made in November of that year. In November and December, Maclear also used his rods to remeasure the Parade Ground Baseline and marked each end with a cannon. This base was provided for land surveyors so that they could compare their chains with an accurately determined distance. The laying out of this baseline created great interest in Cape Town and Piazzi Smyth was again inspired to caricature the scene: Figure 20. His feelings are clearly revealed: Maclear is the only person actually working, Gibbs and the soldier Kirke are drinking, the police are busy "Keeping the ground" by aggressive action towards a small cat, while a spectator harasses Maclear by standing on tiptoe to peer at his notes. The contemporary Cape attitude towards gentlemen visiting on their way to India is shown in the indolence of the "Indian Spectators", and Piazzi's attitude towards church elders is indicated by the pompous caption.

With these exercises behind him, Maclear was prepared for an expedition to Klipfontein for the purpose of locating the northern end of Lacaille's arc.

Herschel was keen to accompany him but could not, owing to the short time left before he returned to England. Maclear postponed his journey so that he could be in Cape Town to wish the Herschels bon voyage.

In his four years at the Cape, Herschel had accomplished his aim of surveying the southern sky, discovering in the process some 1 700 nebulae, 2 100 double stars and a miscellany of other astronomical notabilia. He and Maclear had taken great delight in observing the reappearance of Halley's Comet in 1836 and had collaborated in making a series of accurate measurements of its positions. Some of Maclear's observations were made with the 14-feet reflector that had been sitting in its packing case since Fallows's time: Herschel repolished the mirror and Maclear erected the telescope on the wooden floor under one of the domes. This was the first employment of the "extra-meridian" facilities and proved to be a serious failure, not because of the telescope, which Herschel described as having "fine light and a very good defining power", but because no instrument piers had been provided for mounting the telescopes. Maclear's opinion was "These domes have been foolishly placed absolutely resting on a floor, a wooden floor, over a room nearly 20 feet square belonging to the dwelling house and no Pillar, nothing but the said floor for the Instrument... The plan is ludicrously foolish, an instrument upon which such important observations depend to be placed on a boarded floor and that on the upper storey! with a violent wind".

The departure of the Herschels, in the Windsor on 11 March 1838, left an unfillable gap in the life of the Maclears. Although of different characters

1. Mr Maclear. 2. Major Mitchell. 3. Lt Williams. 4. Mr Hertzog. 5. Gibbs Carpenter.
8 Cape Spectators. 9 Indian Spectators. 10 Members of an Extra-provisional-de
Right Venerable the Synod of the Ecclesiastical Courts of the Dutch Reformed

and backgrounds, Herschel and Maclear had thrived on mutual assistance. Herschel the eminent polymath - the heart of British science, transplanted to South Africa - interested in everything around him, yet able to knuckle down to the tedious task of observing on almost every clear night. Maclear, the Irish amateur, launched into a new career, determined to make his name, anxious that Herschel should carry home a favourable impression - "The reason why you [Herschel] should judge for yourself rather than from my report is obvious (I have a character to get)" - willing to undertake surveys of dimensions that would daunt a less tenacious spirit. They worked and parted with strong friendship and mutual respect. This was to be of great importance for the future of the Observatory.

Herschel went home to a Baronetcy at the coronation of Queen Victoria, and public expression of esteem and reverence. His sense of obligation to serve the public led him to accept a multitude of offices that frustrated him to distraction - writing to Maclear in July 1844 he said "I have never mourned over quitting the Cape - but once - and that mourning began the day I left it and has lasted till now - and ten times in the year I more than half resolved to quit England with my family for ever, and come back within sight of the good old Table Hill". However, his influence in British science was without equal - even Airy considered Herschel primus inter pares - and, as we shall see, he was to use this power to further the interests of the Observatory.

Herschel had made a considerable impact on Cape Society; when Maclear proposed that a permanent monument be erected to commemorate his residence, he found ready support. After a "newspaper war" between two factions who

20
Measurement of the Parade Baseline, by C.P. Smyth (detail)

differed in their opinions as to the best site, Maclear's party triumphed (their rivals argued for the Grand Parade) and a hollow obelisk was erected over the small granite cylinder left by Herschel to mark the centre of his great telescope at Feldhausen. When Herschel sold Feldhausen, he retained a piece of land sixty-three feet in diameter, centred on the granite cylinder, and this remained in the family until it was transferred, by a great-granddaughter of Sir John, to the City of Cape Town during the Herschel Centenary celebrations in 1934. The inscriptions that are now seen on the obelisk were fixed there in 1905 and were designed and supplied by three sons of Sir John and a son of Maclear.

Herschel's beneficial influence began immediately on his return to England. On 29 June 1838 he sent a long letter to Sir Francis Beaufort; the proposals contained in this letter assured the expansion of the Observatory over the next ten years. As a result of these propositions, Herschel and Francis Baily were requested to apply to the Government for additional telescopes and another Assistant for the Cape Observatory. These were granted.

The Second Assistant, William Mann, arrived at the Cape on 22 October 1839, bringing with him some of the instruments required for the remeasurement of Lacaille's Arc of Meridian. Mann was the third son of Major General Cornelius Mann, commander of the Royal Engineers at Gibraltar. He celebrated his twenty-second birthday three days after landing at the Cape and was thus a year older than Piazzi Smyth. Mann, although colour-blind, was an artist; he and Smyth became firm friends.

Another of Herschel's contributions involved the Mural Circle. Maclear had proposed to the Admiralty that the Circle be exchanged for the one at Greenwich. There were in fact two such instruments at Greenwich - the one by Jones originally destined for the Cape had been intercepted by Pond and mounted alongside the earlier Troughton Circle. Airy, appointed Astronomer Royal in 1836 in succession to Pond, did not continue the double-instrument technique developed by Pond and, on Herschel's recommendation, agreed to the transfer of the Circle. It arrived at the Cape in July 1839, was immediately mounted in place of the old Circle, and a delighted Maclear wrote to Airy to say that "you can conceive the practical gratification in having opposite readings [of the microscopes] within a second or two - to an observer who never witnessed such a phenomenon".

On its arrival in England, Airy sent the Cape Mural Circle to the instrument-maker William Simms, "and after some examination of its large pivot, which was evidently deformed, Mr Simms proceeded under my direction to re-turn it, when, to our great astonishment, the steel collar of the pivot was found quite loose, having been attached merely by soft solder". The usual method of fitting the collar was to make it slightly undersize and then to expand it with heat, fix it while hot and thus obtain a firm joint. The sloppy workmanship of this instrument, which frustrated the first decade of observing at the Cape, most probably came from an assistant when Jones's back was turned. Airy went on to say that "there is not the smallest appearance of mechanical injury to the instrument", thereby releasing Fallows from any responsibility for injury during unloading at Cape Town jetty.

From late 1837 until 1847, Maclear, Smyth and Mann were heavily engaged in work on the Arc of Meridian. The triangulation measurements were made with the most accurate theodolites available: one, contributed by Sir Francis Beaufort, was never returned and is now housed in the South African Museum. The very accurate latitude measurements, required at each end of the Arc, could only be achieved with the aid of a Zenith Sector. As the one intended for the centre room of the Observatory had never been constructed, Maclear borrowed one from England. The Sector sent to him was, even at that time, an historic instrument: that used by James Bradley in 1727 for observations which resulted in the discovery of the aberration of light. Airy was reluctant to release this instrument but, with Herschel's assurances, decided to entrust it to Maclear. It arrived in Cape Town on 9 December 1837.

Bradley's Sector was a fragile and ungainly instrument $12\frac{1}{2}$ feet long and mounted in a vertical position. In order to erect it, Maclear had to modify the Lantern on the Observatory roof. After some practice with the Sector, Maclear moved it to the backyard of Mrs De Witt's house at 2 Strand Street and positioned it as near as possible to Lacaille's original site. Strong wind and blowing sand made observations unprofitable so, having observed for the first three weeks of February 1838, the Sector was moved to a site on the north front of Table Mountain at the bottom of Platteklip Gorge. The observations made there from 24 February to 13 March were intended as an experiment to see by how much the mass of Table Mountain affected the latitude determination.

Abandoning further work in Cape Town, on 15 March Maclear, Smyth, Lieutenant Williams, Joseph Gibbs and four other men set off for the northern end of Lacaille's Arc at Klipfontein. They were unable to identify the exact position of Lacaille's observation station; they erected the Sector on a nearby site on the same farm. In the field the Sector was housed in a tent, 13 feet high, specially made for the purpose. High winds and, later in the survey, freezing rain and snow caused endless trouble with this tent.

Observations at Klipfontein were completed by 22 April and the Sector was returned to Cape Town. There it was erected in the Rogge Bay Guard House, near to Strand Street but better protected from the wind. On 30 June it was again moved to the Observatory.

Triangulation of the Arc required a Baseline and extensive surveys. A Baseline was laid out as near as possible to that of Lacaille, which was no longer discernible and therefore could not be checked. The operations for this Baseline, a little over eight miles in length, were more demanding than in Lacaille's time, and lasted from 21 October 1840 until 5 April 1841. During this period, Maclear had the assistance of Captain Alexander Henderson and a party of eight other Royal Engineers who had been sent out from England. He was also provided with 14 men from the Garrison in Cape Town. Maclear and Smyth superintended the operations and made all of the crucial measurements themselves.

The survey work necessitated a great deal of mountaineering. The theodolites, and the heliostats (solar reflectors) used for signalling and sighting the theodolites, were hauled to the tops of several mountains which would give a clear view from one station to the next. Much of the assistance in this work came from survivors of the wreck of the Abercrombie Robinson on 28 August 1842, which "threw several persons out of work, who having no local ties were ready for a bush life, and gladly accepted service on the Survey".

After repeating the measurement of Lacaille's Arc of Meridian, Maclear pushed the survey further north and south. The Sector was conveyed to Heerenlogement Berg and Kamies Berg in 1842 and in 1844 to Zwart Kop (south of Simon's Town) and to Cape Point. Work with this instrument was completed in January 1845 and it was sent back to England on 1 May 1850. Maclear was justifiably proud of having returned the Sector in good condition. Modern visitors to the Royal Observatory at Greenwich look with interest at this famous instrument; they could well be encouraged to reflect with admiration on the stamina and determination of Maclear and his team who struggled with this ungainly instrument through the inhospitable terrain of the Western Cape.

The fruits of the Survey were twofold. Firstly, Lacaille's work was vindicated; his measurements had been accurate and his anomalous result was indeed owing to non-allowance for the gravitational attractions of mountains. As it happened, the principal attraction was at the Klipfontein end of his Arc; Table Mountain, although more massive, lies to one side of the Arc and therefore has less influence. The second result was provision of the first "modern" survey of the Cape Colony, upon which all later surveys were able

to build. In the world of surveyors, Maclear is recognised as the founding father of South Africa's trigonometric survey.

Although the demands of the survey were heavy, at least one person had to remain at the Observatory, continuing the routine of meridian observations, and occasionally pursuing some more exciting quarry. In 1843, for example, a bright comet prompted Smyth to dust off the 14-feet reflector - "the brass portions were thickly encrusted with verdigris" and on March 25 he "tried with a piece of rock crystal and an interposed film of mica or sulphate of lime, to determine after Arago's manner, whether the light from the Comet was polarized...". But the next day came a directive from the survey: "Orders have just been received from Mr Maclear ordering 'that all enquiries of a physical description with regard to the Comet are to be thrown overboard; that the 14 feet reflector is to be replaced in the Telescope room; and that nothing is to be done but the determining the place of the Comet'". Piazzi's frustration is evinced by his careful recording of this statement in the observing book - Maclear was conservative and wanted no independent experimentation carried out in his observatory; he well justified the epithet "The Emperor" used in private by Smyth and Mann. Incidentally, from about 1843 on, Smyth had been pioneering photography in South Africa (with assistance from correspondence with Herschel). His calotypes, recently discovered in the archives at the Royal Greenwich Observatory and at the Royal Society of Edinburgh, provide the earliest extant photographic illustrations of Cape scenes.

21 The Royal Observatory, lithograph by C.F. Angas (detail)

A new and, to Maclear, unwelcome addition to the Observatory buildings appeared in 1841. At the instigation of General Edward Sabine, supported, among others, by Herschel, a global network of magnetic and meteorological observatories was established, including one in the grounds of the Royal Observatory run by a detachment of the Royal Artillery. The group that arrived on 18 March 1840 in the ships Erebus and Terror, of Captain James Clark Ross's Antarctic Expedition, included three non-commissioned officers and two other ranks, led by Lieutenant Frederick Eardley-Wilmot. They erected a cottage, a dwelling house for the men, a magnetic observatory built of wood with copper and brass fittings, a "Wind Tower" supporting an anenometer, and several smaller huts to house the various bits of magnetic apparatus. The whole ensemble was sited in the south-east corner of the Observatory grounds, away from the meridian views of the principal instruments (Figure 21). This piece of land was part of an extension of the original small parallelogram obtained by Fallows: Maclear acquired the extra land in 1840 in exchange for the more distant pieces of Government property procured by Fallows. The presence of so many dwelling houses at the Observatory had one salutary effect: in 1842 the Admiralty sanctioned the expense of building a wooden bridge across the Liesbeek, which was designed and erected by John Skirrow. Although the magnetic observatory was run by the Army, with independent funds from the Treasury, Maclear expressed concern that the stated period of three years for which the site was requested would be extended under his own supervision. His well-founded suspicions were based on the large expenditure incurred in establishing the magnetic observatory - £4 242 appeared too much to be abandoned after so short a time. His fears were confirmed in July 1846 when the buildings and duties were transferred to the Admiralty and Maclear received instructions to continue the work, albeit on a reduced scale. In the transfer, Maclear received a third Assistantship, initially filled by George Roberts Smalley, who resigned in October 1851 to become Professor of Mathematics at the South African College. He was replaced by Pierce Morton (a Cambridge mathematician and one-time student of Airy). The Assistants were thus of high calibre, but nevertheless in a letter to Airy in 1849 Maclear bemoans the fact that "the Magnetic observatory necessarily occupies a large portion of my time and attention".

The buildings associated with the magnetic observatory substantially altered the appearance of the Royal Observatory on its southern side. The Wind Tower, a copy of the Tower of Winds in Athens, was considered very picturesque and appropriate to the Grecian style of the main building. The principal laboratory (second building to the left of the Wind Tower in Figure 21) was consumed by fire on 12 March 1852 and was replaced by a smaller one in 1859. Less attention was paid to magnetic work after 1857; the Assistant and the buildings gradually became used for astronomical purposes. After Maclear's retirement in 1869, no further magnetic work was carried out, but meteorological observations continued.

To return to events in the 1840's, in the early part of 1845 Piazzi Smyth, now twenty-six years old, with the aid of a strong supporting letter from Herschel was appointed to succeed Thomas Henderson at Edinburgh. Henderson had died on 23 November 1844, leaving most of his Cape and Edinburgh observations unpublished. Before setting off to take up his position as Astronomer Royal for Scotland, Smyth volunteered to help Maclear complete an important part of the survey work. He eventually sailed on 22 October 1845.

During his decade at the Cape, Smyth had made invaluable contributions to Maclear's success in the surveys and in the routine meridian observations. Under his own name, he had so far published only an article on Astronomical Drawing in the Memoirs of the Royal Astronomical Society, and - ever an opportunist - a note on the stability of wooden floors for telescope mounts! On the surveys he had worked meticulously and untiringly, often under conditions of physical hardship - he spent the winter of 1845 on the summit of snow-covered Sniewkop in the Hottentots Holland mountain range, during which one of his party died of exposure.

He was responsible for one radical change in the appearance of the Observatory, of which he was justifiably proud. In 1852 he published a description in the Practical Mechanics Journal. The bareness of the Observatory hill, "exposed to a hot sun and a fierce wind, blowing, too, almost invariably in the direction of the meridian, to the great detriment of many important observations of close south polar stars", Piazzi saw as a challenge and he was determined to provide a covering of trees. The local farmers claimed that the

22   Sketch from scrapbook of Charles Midgley (detail)

dry summers made growth impossible on such a site, but in 1836 Piazzi had a pump sent out from England and fitted it to a windmill of his own design. "Then began its pumping operations, and they were continued ever after during my residence at the Cape, pumping up to the top of the hill a continuous stream of about 400 gallons an hour". Most of the water appears to have been used for Smyth's own garden outside the East (Assistant's) Wing of the Observatory: "so completely was the character of the hill altered from its dried and windy condition formerly, to its sheltered and watered state now, that bananas, of all trees requiring most water and shelter, grew, and produced fruit before I left". Not all of the exotic horticulture was reserved for Smyth: in the diary of Mary, thirteen year old daughter of the Maclears, for 21 July 1840 we find the entry "Mr. Smyth gave me for my garden, two Loquats, a Bay, 3 Figs and a Tea plant". Sketches made after about 1842, show the tremendous increase in arboreal growth on the East side of the Observatory (Figure 22). After the fire of 1852 Maclear followed suit and installed a larger pump and windmill in a ditch running from the Liesbeek River, which was used mainly for filling two large water reservoirs sunk in the ground to the north of the Observatory. Smyth's pump in the Salt River was still working in the 1850's. Smyth's character, and eccentricity, are well summarised in a letter written to Mrs Maclear by Eardly-Wilmot, after he and Mann had visited Smyth in Edinburgh in 1847: "Mann will tell you all about Smyth, his old style of indifference to any personal comfort remains. His house is furnished with considerable taste; but he appears perfectly indifferent as to whether he eats or drinks or sleeps - they all appear to be necessary interruptions which he makes as short as possible". A self-portrait, made this same year, is reproduced in Figure 17.

When Piazzi Smyth left the Cape he took with him impressions of the Observatory which ten years later he communicated to Airy; these throw some light on certain inadequacies in the design of the main building: "in place of the observing rooms being alone, & sacred & commanding all the convenience & means & appliances for making observations nicely and correctly that might easily be obtained when an obsy is to be built de nova; they are pestered with the domestic part of the structure. Two doors open from either wing with the transit & circle rooms: the only covered communication between the two wings is through all three observing rooms; & spite of occasional strong attempts to stop this passage it was always being used... The passages connecting every room on the ground floor of either wing were parts of the same flooring as that of the transit room & circle room: and the passages which connected similarly all the rooms of the upper floors of the wings were fixed against, & into, the upper part of the walls of the transit room (these being much higher than the wing rooms). The consequence is, that while there may be a family of no more than ordinarily rackety children, transit observations are continually interfered with for 12 hours of the 24, a noise in the passage being almost as loud as if made in the room; they find their way in & play with the mercury [in the artificial horizon troughs], & at hide & seek behind the instruments, & up & down the steps".

In Edinburgh, Piazzi Smyth completed Henderson's work and made numerous meridian observations of his own. He also continued to pioneer in photography, publishing the first book illustrated with stereoscopic pictures and constructing a remarkable miniature camera. He became an outspoken advocate of mountain tops for the sites of large observatories - a consequence of his experiences in the Cape ranges - and (partly in collaboration with A.S.Herschel, one of Sir John's sons) was recognised as a leading spectroscopist. His reputation suffered, and continues to suffer, from his enthusiastic involvement in metrology of the Great Pyramid, a subject in which even Herschel became embroiled.

With Smyth's resignation, Maclear appointed William Mann to First Assistant, a position that he held until December 1872. A few months after Smyth departed, Mann fell from his horse and suffered severe head injuries which impaired his health for the rest of his life. As a consequence of his fall, Maclear was obliged to send Mann to England for treatment and recuperation and on this occasion he wrote "I feel the loss of Mr Mann's services, especially at the present juncture. His powerful intellect, his unflinching integrity, and his industry enable me to trust him with confidence on all occasions and in every department, whether at the observatory or on the triangulation, being certain that whatever is practicable he will accomplish, and that what he does will be sure to be well done". This high opinion helped Mann in his most formidable task - he succeeded in 1854 in gaining permission to marry Caroline, Maclear's second daughter.

Briefly continuing with Assistants, on Mann's promotion, the Reverend George Childe was appointed Second Assistant. When he resigned in May 1852 (the second to become a Professor of Mathematics at the South African College) Maclear appointed his own son, George William Herschel Maclear, who served as Second Assistant until June 1893. The origin of his names is obvious; another son was called Thomas Henderson Maclear.

Further subsidiary buildings in the grounds of the Observatory rose in the late 1840's. The impossibility of using the domes provided for "extra-meridian" observations compelled Maclear to use his auxiliary telescopes - the fourteen feet reflector, a 3-inch refractor by Dollond and a $3\frac{1}{2}$-inch by Jones - in the open air. In January 1844 Maclear erected a make-shift dome for the 3-inch, "A square building of wood supported on 4 cast iron wheels and rotating on a brick railway even with the common surface of the ground...to the North of the Mural Circle...the frame work is covered with $\frac{1}{4}$ inch deal, with roof shutters in the ordinary way...the area of the square building is 8 feet square". This was replaced in 1847 by a permanent, circular stone building with a rotating wooden roof and shutter. The 3-inch telescope, which may appear small by modern standards, but about which Maclear waxed enthusiastic: "It is the work of Mr Dollond, and is certainly the most perfect of its dimensions I have met with" was mounted equatorially in the "English" style, i.e. with north and south piers, built of stone, and a polar axis $7\frac{1}{2}$ feet in length. The dome was built 52 yards north of the East Wing.

Two years after this structure was finished, another was erected, 14 feet in diameter, in an almost symmetrical setting, 53 yards to the north of the West Wing. The framework for the dome was sent out from England, overlooked when the vessel docked at the Cape, and finally retrieved from Madras after a trip of seven months' duration! It rotated on three cannon balls and housed a 7-inch refractor built by Merz of Munich. Herschel was almost singlehandedly responsible for having this magnificent telescope sent out to Maclear and had recommended it to the Admiralty in his 1838 letter - he was anxious that the double stars that he had discovered in 1834-1838 should be reobserved with an instrument of adequate power. Several attempts were made to find an English instrument of high quality; Simms offered an 8-inch lens which Herschel rejected after exhaustive tests - his lengthy report (which could have served as a practical manual of lens testing, written by the leading authority of the nineteenth century) demonstrates the labour that he was willing to undertake for the sake of the Observatory.

It was Maclear's intention to erect another dome, for the $3\frac{1}{2}$-inch refractor, roughly midway between these two new domes. The site was prepared, but there is no evidence that a building was erected. The telescope itself was converted into a collimator for the Transit Circle (see below).

The charming sketch (Figure 22) by an unknown artist, contained in the scrapbook of Charles Midgley is dated c.1840. We see from the absence of the 3-inch telescope dome and the presence of luxuriant foliage in Piazzi Smyth's garden that a more probable date is 1845. The function of the small thatched hut contiguous to the (1836) stable has not been established.

The Observatory in the 1850's appears in several of Bowler's watercolours. The one reproduced here (Figure 23) gives a good impression of the general situation of the Observatory. The 3-inch telescope dome is just visible, but the 7-inch dome is lost against a background of trees. The Time Ball is shown in a raised position; it could only be seen thus from 12.55 p.m. when it was

23   Watercolour by Thomas Bowler, 1854 (detail)

hoisted until it was dropped precisely at 1.00 p.m. In October 1853 a Post Office Notice was published informing the shipping world that "As the observatory time signal is not visible from the whole of Table Bay Anchorage, a Time Ball has been established at the Lion's Rump Signal station so as to command the entire sweep of the Bay"; a man with a telescope on Lion's Rump watched the Observatory Time Ball and released his own Ball "as near as possible at the instant when the observatory Ball begins to drop". In October 1857 Maclear arranged for a Time Ball to be established at Simon's Town; the time was determined by a portable transit instrument loaned by the Observatory. The steady growth of trees on the Observatory hill eventually obscured the Time Ball, so on 21 May 1860 Maclear relocated it to the north, on the site intended for the $3\frac{1}{2}$-inch telescope. From September 1861 the telegraph wires, recently established between Cape Town and Simon's Town and which passed close by the Observatory, were used to send electric impulses to cause automatic release of the three Time Balls. To power his signals, Maclear used batteries housed in a hut next to the 7-inch telescope dome. This battery hut was the wooden dip house from the magnetic observatory, transferred to its new site in May 1860. In June 1863 the Time Ball was again moved, being then placed on a wooden pyramidal tower erected against the north wall of the old stables. By 26 August 1865 Maclear was able to announce that "at the instant of one o'clock, the time-ball clock closed the circuit, when the Observatory ball, the Simon's Town ball, the Cape Town time-gun, and the Port Elizabeth ball, were discharged success-

fully, a feat perhaps without parallel in electric work, considering that Port Elizabeth is distant 500 miles from the observatory".

The elegant gouache and pastel study by an unknown artist (Figure 24) can be dated between May 1860 and June 1863 from the existence of the northern flagstaff but absence of the Time Ball tower. Apart from variations in tree coverage, the Observatory changed little in appearance over the next twenty years. A map of the site as it was in 1863 is given in Figure 25.

One other instrumental change occurred during Maclear's reign; this was the introduction of a Transit Circle. The Transit Instrument and Mural Circle installed at the Cape followed the British tradition of using these separate instruments for accurate positional work. On the Continent, however, a Transit Circle was generally used, which combined the functions of the two instruments and made it easier to reduce the results. As early as 1822 Fallows had requested a Transit Circle instead of the proposed instruments, but he was ignored. In 1847, Airy proposed that a large Transit Circle should be installed at Greenwich, and produced a design of such outstanding merit that the instrument was an immediate success on its completion in 1850. Quite naturally, Maclear wanted an equally powerful tool and, with the support of Airy and Herschel, succeeded in persuading the Admiralty to give him a duplicate of Airy's telescope. William Mann was sent to England on 9 October 1852 to learn the mechanical details of the Transit Circle and to be instructed in the method of mounting it; he returned on 22 December 1853, having assisted in packing the instrument before he left England. The various pieces of the Transit Circle arrived at the Cape in February and March 1854.

24   The Royal Observatory, by an unknown artist (detail)

The new instrument, built by Troughton and Simms,* was mounted in the room previously occupied by the Mural Circle, so it was necessary to "lengthen the room meridian wise from 24 ft. to about 36 ft., by carrying out the North wall to the N.E. corner of the adjoining computing room". This destroyed the perfect symmetry of the main building - and forfeited one of the cherished water-closets. The old Mural Circle pier was demolished (during which Fallows's document of October 1828 was discovered and reinstated) and replaced by two stone piers, the lower courses of which were constructed from the stones of the Mural pier (including the eleven ton goliath), and the upper courses with a white sandstone obtained from Tygerberg quarry. Considerable delay occurred because "no stonemasons were available : the few who had resisted the temptation of the Australian gold-fields, were engaged at advanced wages by builders in Cape Town". At the start of 1855, however, Maclear was pleased to report that "Throughout this business, viz. the building of the upper part of the West pier and the mounting of the instrument, the working engineer was my first Assistant, Mr Mann, to whom I am indebted for effecting the whole without an accident, or a single circumstance to regret". Observations with the Transit Circle (Figure 26) commenced on 27 January 1855.

*In 1826 the ageing Edward Troughton entered into partnership with William Simms. In 1922 the firm amalgamated with the optical company of Thomas Cooke and became the present Cooke, Troughton and Simms.

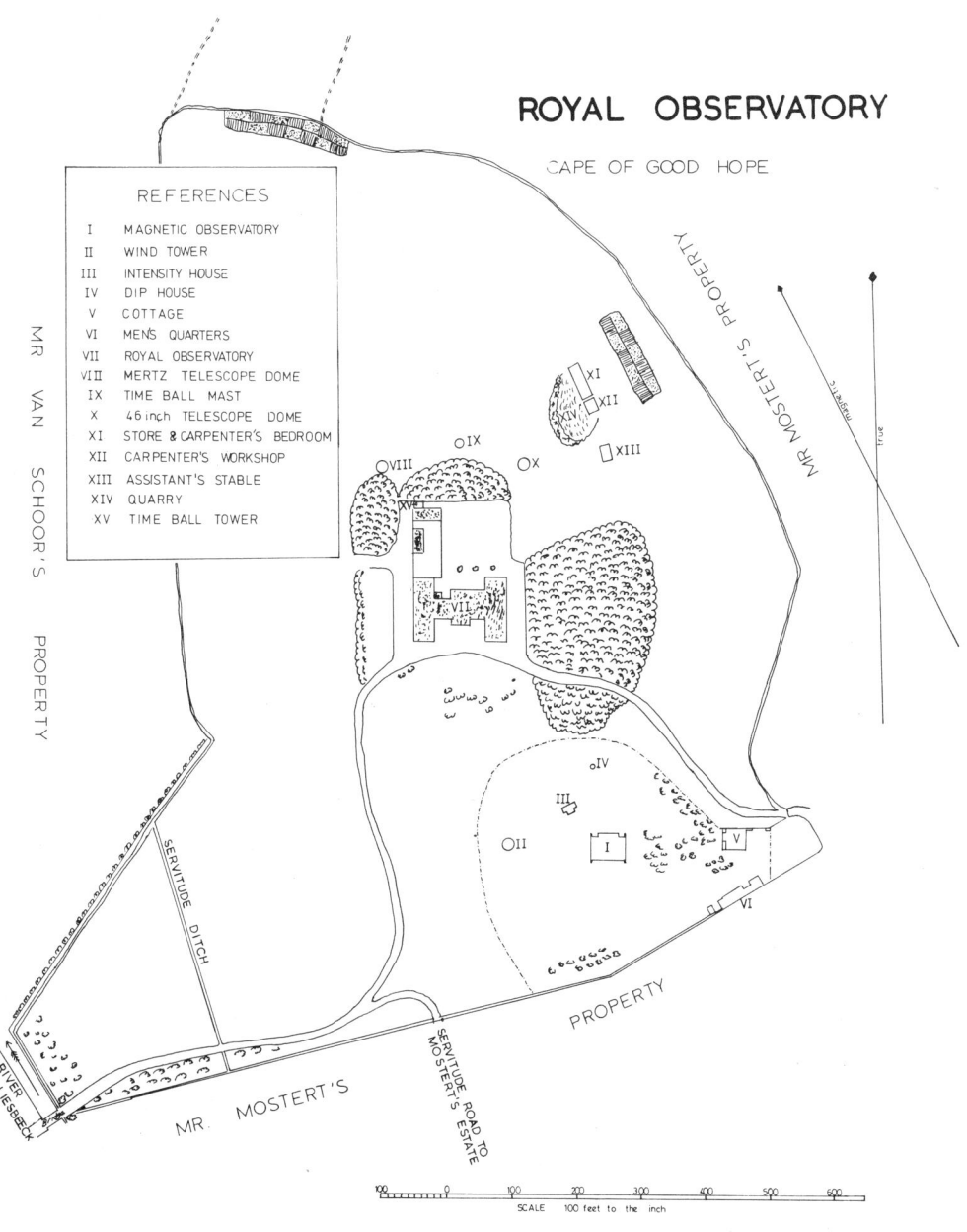

25   Map of the Royal Observatory, 1863

26 *The Transit Circle*

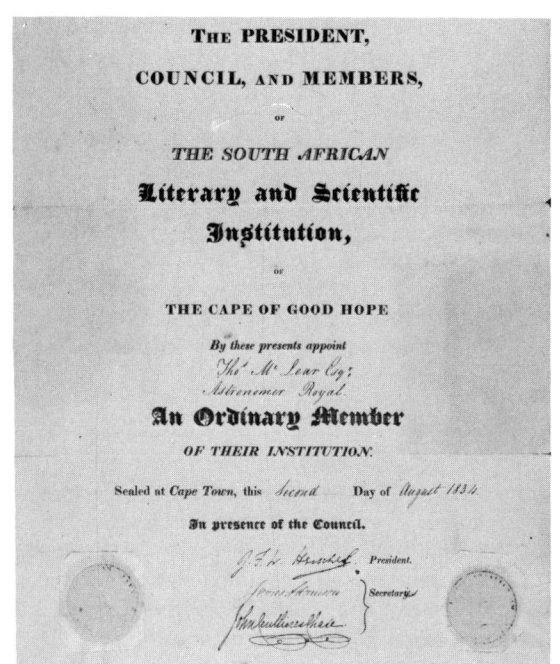

27

Thomas Maclear's membership form for the South African Literary and Scientific Association

Maclear's extra-mural (one is tempted to say extra-Transit) activities were multifarious throughout his professional career. He was an active member of the South African Literary and Scientific Institution (the old S.A. Institution, renamed in 1832) from the day of his election on 2 August 1834:- the day that Herschel was elected President (see Figure 27). The following year he became a Freemason at the English Lodge, in which he rose to Deputy Principal Grand Master. He served many years on the examining body of the South African College, was a Trustee of the South African Museum from 1855 until 1870, and acted as chairman of the Building Committee as well as a Trustee of the South African Library. He was also active on the Coast Light Commission, the Weights and Measures Commission and other lesser bodies.

These numerous activities led to his becoming perhaps the best-known figure in Cape Town, but they detracted from his astronomical activities. The labours of reducing the Arc of Meridian observations also severely retarded his astronomical computations; although the field work for the survey was completed in 1847, the two great volumes entitled "Verification and Extension of La Caille's Arc of Meridian at the Cape of Good Hope" did not appear until 1866. In 1840 Maclear had published the Transit and Mural observations made during his first year at the Cape and in the Introduction to that work apologizes for the large number of errata, saying "However nothing in future will be sent to press without systematic revision". In an annotated copy in the possession of the Royal Observatory, one of Maclear's successors has obliterated the last three words in the quoted sentence and comments sarcastically in the margin.

This pointedly illustrates the dissatisfaction felt in many quarters over Maclear's apparent tardiness in producing the catalogue of southern stars requested in his initial Instructions. Airy made repeated requests in the 1850's and 1860's for this catalogue and his private correspondence contains numerous strictures on Maclear's neglect. In defence, it must be allowed that Maclear was provided with very little assistance in the arduous work of reduction and preparation of his observations for the press and that he recognised the importance of securing observations at that epoch, rather than abandoning these in favour of a catalogue. He did in fact make a great deal of progress in that direction before his retirement.

Maclear's labours did not go unrewarded. In June 1860, five months after he returned from his only visit to England (which also encompassed Ireland, Paris and Brussels) he received the accolade for his services to astronomy: he was well aware that this knighthood owed a great deal to the friendship of Herschel and fully expressed his appreciation. The Maclears did not long enjoy their enhanced status: Lady Maclear's health declined shortly after Maclear's return and on 27 July 1861 she expired, causing Maclear great anguish. Maclear received permission for a piece of the Observatory ground to be set aside for burial of astronomers and their families, and in this plot, not far from Fallows's grave, he interred his wife.

The publication of his Arc of Meridian opus brought acclaim from the scientific community: the Lalande Medal of the French Institute in 1867 and a Gold Medal of the Royal Society in 1869.

Exploration was a lifelong interest of Maclear's, being perhaps one of the principal stimuli for his extension of the Arc of Meridian into the wilds of the Western Cape. Together with Herschel, he had served on the Committee of the Association for Exploring Central Africa, and had become a close friend of the Association's leader (and earlier associate of Fallows), Andrew Smith. Both Fallows and Maclear at various times lent Smith chronometers, thermometers and sextants. In 1850 Maclear met David Livingstone, instructed him in the use of the sextant, and commenced a lifelong intimate friendship. During his explorations, Livingstone wrote many long letters to Maclear and sent his sextant and chronometer observations for reduction - another task that encroached upon Maclear's time. On one of his visits, Livingstone presented Maclear with a rhinoceros hide walking stick, which is still in the possession of the Observatory.

In 1868 Airy suggested to Maclear that he should consider retirement, but abandoned further action when Maclear responded that he would stand down only for his son-in-law William Mann (who had received distinction in 1863 by the offer of the "Astronomership at Sydney", which he declined). The following year, Airy corresponded with the Naval Hydrographer Captain G.H. Richards, soliciting his opinion on the advisability of Maclear being replaced. Richards's concurrence was ironically reinforced by a chance meeting described in Airy's letter to Richards of 10 November 1869: "A short time since, one of my assistants accidentally fell in with a Mr Bowler, who (I believe) was Maclear's assistant in 1832 [sic] and for a short time, and who has lately returned from the Cape of Good Hope. He reported that Maclear is very feeble. I suppose that the idea of making Maclear's retirement depend on a family arrangement cannot be entertained. I entirely assent to your proposition that new blood is always desirable. I say also young blood, a man at the age 32 to 35, with proper education, is best". Airy was seven years Maclear's junior, and had himself been 34 years old when appointed Astronomer Royal; he remained in that post until his eightieth year.

With Airy's backing, Richards sent a letter to Maclear on 10 January 1870 diplomatically informing him that "Most of the Civil Departments of the Government have lately been undergoing reorganization, and the Heads and other officers belonging to them who have reached a certain age have been advised to retire, and among other Institutions the Cape Observatory has not been overlooked". He continued with praise of Maclear's work, and an invitation that "you should address me on the subject and request that I bring your application for retirement under the consideration of their Lordships". Maclear capitulated with grace.

Although one of his sons-in-law offered the use of a large house adjoining the Observatory grounds, Maclear wisely resolved to avoid interfering in the affairs of his successor and took up residence at Grey Villa, a house in Mowbray. Nevertheless, reduction of his observations took him frequently to the Observatory. On 11 May 1871 Herschel died; one of his last letters was written to Maclear, who was greatly distressed by the death of his, and the Observatory's, old friend. At about this time, Maclear's eyesight began to deteriorate, which terminated his computations. By 1876 he was totally blind. He was lovingly attended by his family, particularly his unmarried daughter Mary. His interest in exploration continued to the end; the last occasion on which he left Grey Villa was to meet H.M.Stanley and his appearance in public "was received with even greater applause than that which greeted Stanley himself". Only a month before his death, Maclear was visited by David Gill (whom we will be meeting in Chapter 5) who reported that "to his latest days he spoke of Sir John Herschel and his times, and of all the work and of all the fun they had together, with a racy enthusiasm but seldom met with in one beyond the years of middle life, and still more seldom in a man bereft of sight and on his last sick bed".

Maclear breathed his last on 14 July 1879 and was buried beside his wife in the grounds of the Observatory. On 17 July, the House of Assembly in Cape Town resolved "That this House desires to express its deep sense of the signal services rendered by the late Sir Thomas Maclear, Knt., F.R.S., F.R.A.S., to the general cause of astronomical and geographical science while in charge of the Royal Observatory, Cape Town, and also to the material interests of the colony in the practical application of his researches; and, furthermore, its high appreciation of his devotion for so long a period of years to the cause of South African exploration and civilisation, and that this resolution be recorded in the journals of the House".

Maclear's name is still in evidence: the town of Maclear in the Cape Province, Cape Maclear and Maclear's Beach at the southernmost tip of the Cape Peninsula, Maclear's Beacon on Table Mountain, Cape Maclear on the southern shore of Lake Malawi (formerly Lake Nyasa), a minor road in Cape Town and a bridge in Bain's Kloof pass all ensure that his name lives on in Africa.

4 Edward James Stone
1870-1879

The choice of a successor to Maclear was governed by one exigency: preparation of the catalogue of southern stars that had been requested nearly forty years earlier. A man would be required who was willing to work over the backlog of Cape observations and be able to extend the measurements to fainter stars with the aid of the Transit Circle. The Chief Assistant of the Royal Greenwich Observatory was just such a person: experienced with the Transit Circle (twin of the one at the Cape) and well versed in the niceties of meridian astronomy. Airy had no reluctance in parting with his principal assistant, if it meant that the southern catalogue would at last appear; he had almost given up hope of seeing it in his lifetime.

Edward James Stone was born in London on 28 February 1831. He was a sickly youth and spent most of his early years with relatives in Devon. He showed no particular predilection for study until his late teens. At the age of twenty his ability at mathematics became apparent and he was persuaded to become a student at King's College, London. His progress was rapid and in 1855 he entered Queen's College, Cambridge. Continual ill health frustrated his studies but in 1859 he graduated as Fifth Wrangler. Shortly afterwards he was elected a Fellow of his College.

In 1860 the Revd Robert Main, Airy's Chief Assistant at Greenwich, was appointed to the post of Radcliffe Observer at Oxford (in succession to Manuel Johnson) and Airy selected Stone to fill the vacancy. As was often the case with Greenwich appointments, the new Chief Assistant arrived with little or no practical experience of astronomy, which necessitated instruction from the seasoned members of staff, many of whom were more than twice his age. Although he quickly mastered the techniques of practical astronomy, his lack of practical inclination, and inability to tolerate night work, led Stone to follow his talents in the theoretical field.

During his ten years at Greenwich, Stone accomplished an impressive quantity of original research. His principal interest lay in what Airy termed "the noblest problem in astronomy" - that of deriving the distance of the Earth from the Sun. Stone rediscussed the available published measurements that were relevant to this problem. Included in these were accurate positions of Mars contributed by Maclear. He also redetermined the distance of the Moon by comparing observations made at Greenwich and at the Cape. The success of these investigations was recognised by his election to the Royal

Society in 1868 and award of the Gold Medal of the Royal Astronomical Society in 1869.

Stone was as aware as Airy of the lacuna in the southern hemisphere. He later stated that "The chief inducement which led me to accept the appointment was the opportunity which the position afforded for the formation of a general catalogue of Southern stars...". His enthusiasm for this task, and the esteem in which he was held, made him the obvious candidate for the Cape post. He learned of his success in June 1870. Stone, his wife Grace (nee Tuckett, whom he married in 1866) and their one child, sailed for the Cape on board the mail steamer Saxon in September of that year and arrived in Table Bay on 13 October. After staying a short time in a hotel, they took up residence at the Observatory on 22 October.

The observatory that Stone took into his charge was in a state of gradual decay. Apart from the Time Ball tower, no construction had been seen for over a decade. Only desultory repairs had been made and the grounds were beginning to run wild. A few months' effort would be required to rejuvenate the establishment, but this Stone chose not to do. From his point of view, he had come to the Cape for one purpose only, and that was catalogue, catalogue, catalogue. Thirty years' backlog of observations and new measurements had to be reduced. Stone approached the task single-mindedly: during working hours he and his staff progressed towards the catalogue; after hours, Stone occupied himself by working even harder at the same task. In his decade at the Observatory he allowed few distractions from the main objective; he judged wisely, for the work was barely finished when he left.

From a personal point of view, Stone found his first weeks at the Observatory distinctly uncomfortable. The following extracts from the letter he wrote to Airy on 17 June 1871 illuminate the problems:

Dear Sir,

I must congratulate the KCB's on having you amongst them. [Airy had several times previously declined knighthood]. I am getting on quite comfortably and have complete command over the observatory and staff. My orders are carried out without murmurs audible to me; more I cannot of course answer for. I have had to keep myself rather aloof from Sir Thos Maclear although, I believe, that we are on perfectly friendly terms and I fully recognize his many good and engaging qualities. He was however rather inclined to hang me here and patronise me and naturally enough, on his part, was anxious to force his son prominently forward on terms of equality: this I on my part, equally naturally I presume, did not, under the circumstances, consider desirable for, Mr G.Maclear is not a man of any knowledge or power...

I found when I arrived that my appointment had been made a question of newspaper discussion by some friends of the Maclears and Manns. Sir Thos was regarded here as a great astronomical genius, the equal at least of the Herschels and yourself. Mr Mann was considered as second only to Sir Thos. The observatory was regarded as one of the wonders of the world, and the amount of work done by the observatory as prodigious.

Of me they had never heard and knew nothing except that I had been an assistant at Greenwich like G. Maclear was here. It was not known that I was an University man or had ever done anything or obtained any position at all in England. It was thought however that I had been most unfairly and unjustly appointed instead of Mr Mann, through a piece of red tapeism in England, because Mr Mann happened to be a year or two over fifty...

You will see that on our arrival here we were rather in a hornets' nest. Poor old Sir Thos too could not without a sigh leave off attendance, on one excuse and another, at the observatory nor attempting to interfere when here... I very soon shewed that I would brook no interference in Observatory matters. In this I took my own course without the slightest regard to the opinion of any one here... It was soon found that things were going on and all difficulties began to vanish. There has followed, what you might expect, a reaction and we now have to take care that we are not drawn out into Society more than either of us wish.

You need not fear about my position here. I can hold my own with the greatest ease. I of course shall not be popular, in the same sense that Maclear was popular, when the observatory was open at night to visitors and turned into a show place.

Soon after this, scarlet fever again visited the Observatory. Mann was severely stricken and two of his children succumbed. He retired on grounds of ill health and survived only to 30 April 1873. Stone's failure to promote George Maclear to the vacancy re-established some of the earlier resentments. However, Stone required a First Assistant with as comprehensive a mathematical background as possible; with Airy's assistance he selected William Henry Finlay.

Finlay, born at Liverpool on 17 June 1849, graduated as 33rd Wrangler in 1873, was appointed to the Cape position in April and arrived at the Cape on 21 June 1873. Although inexperienced in astronomy, he rapidly assimilated the methods of reduction and technique of observing and proceeded to take over the work of preparing Maclear's backlog of observations for the press. During the remainder of Stone's tenure at the Cape, Finlay and George Maclear were almost entirely responsible for the working of the Transit Circle. Stone supervised them closely but did not participate in the gruelling night work.

The diversions from the catalogue that he did allow show Stone's wide interests. As well as some theoretical papers (on the applications of theory of probability) his contributions included several of an experimental nature.

While at Greenwich, Stone had pioneered in the new science of stellar spectroscopy. He brought a small spectroscope, made by Browning, to the Cape and during his first year of residence attached it to the 7-inch equatorial. Further effort was postponed when he found the mounting of the telescope to be too weak. In anticipation of the arrival of a larger spectroscope, ordered before he left England, Stone obtained a new mounting for this telescope and installed it in 1874. However the spectroscope itself, if it ever arrived, seems never to have been used.

A more successful venture in 1871 was a determination of the velocity of sound. The telegraph link between the Observatory and the Imhoff Battery time gun was used both to fire the gun and to enable a man near the gun to send a return signal when the sound of the explosion reached him. The difference in time (about thirteen seconds) was registered between this signal and the time when the report of the cannon arrived at the Observatory. This time difference divided into the known distance between the listeners, gave an accurate measurement of the velocity of sound. Corrections for air temperature and wind velocity were conveniently available from readings made on the Wind Tower.

More ambitious was the expedition mounted in 1874 to observe an eclipse of the Sun on 16 April. In order to cause the least amount of interruption to work at the Observatory, Stone took only his wife with him. They steamed to Port Nolloth on one of the copper ore carriers, thence to Klipfontein (not the same place as visited by Lacaille and Maclear) on the mine tramway (newly completed and still drawn by mules). Here Stone set up his telescope in the garden of the cottage of R.T.Hall, engineer in charge of the Cape Copper Company. The Observatory at this time had no portable telescope so Stone had been obliged to borrow a 4-inch refractor from Henry Solomon, a resident of Cape Town. To this he attached his small spectroscope and successfully observed spectra of the chromosphere and corona during the eclipse. It is of interest to note that these observations constituted the first fruitful application of spectroscopy in South Africa. The Hall family assisted in drawing the appearance of the solar corona at the eclipse. These results, together with others received from amateur observers around the country (alerted by a newspaper article contributed by Stone on the importance of carefully executed drawings) were published in the Memoirs of the Royal Astronomical Society.

Shortly before the solar eclipse, Stone received some new magnetic equipment from England and made a few measurements at the Observatory. He took these instruments on the eclipse expedition and produced the first set of magnetic observations to be made in Namaqualand.

Also in 1874, H.M.S.Challenger called at the Cape. The vessel was on its epic thousand day voyage around the world - the first major oceanographic expedition. Second-in-command was John Fiot Lee Pearse Maclear, son of Sir Thomas. Stone reported that "At the request of Captain Nares, of H.M.S.Challenger, facilities were afforded Commander Maclear and Lt. Bromley for making magnetical observations. The magnetic observatory was cleared and placed entirely at the service of Commander Maclear". Jack Maclear later rose to the rank of Admiral. He added one more link between the Herschel and Maclear families by marrying, on 4 June 1878, Julia Herschel, sixth daughter of Sir John and Lady Herschel. This despite parental opposition - John Maclear was an unsophisticated sailor.

By 1875 the number of new reductions and observations made was sufficient to fill several publications. Stone paid a short visit to England to arrange for their printing. While there he was persuaded to assist in an international effort to maintain a constant watch for sunspots. As a result, a De la Rue type photoheliograph made by Dallmeyer arrived at the Cape later that year. With this it was intended to take two photographs of the Sun each day. The instrument was installed in a wooden hut with an attached darkroom near the magnetic observatory. Observations started on 12 February 1876. This building was the only one erected under Stone's direction. After an enthusiastic start, interest waned and very few photographs were actually taken.

The drudgery of the reductions was not to everyone's taste and it is a tribute to Finlay and G. Maclear that they persevered. Stone was not so fortunate with his other assistants and computers. The nature of the work and the remuneration were deterrents: "The salaries of the observatory staff have been fixed much below the Colonial Standard and young men of ability can get appointments under the Colonial Government at higher salaries with less work and less drain upon the brain". Stone's initial salary was £600 per annum - unchanged since 1820. In 1872 it was improved, by annual increments of £15, to a maximum of £700 p.a. The frequent complaints of the junior staff were passed on to the Admiralty and to Airy but to no avail. In consequence, during Stone's time, more than a dozen computing staff resigned, and each replacement had to be trained, with considerable loss of time, by the senior staff. Even the First Assistant, Finlay, felt the need of a higher income; in October 1876 Stone reported to Airy that "whilst I was in England he started taking private pupils for the Survey and other University Examinations. As this system allowed of almost indefinite increase and his receipt from this source depended upon the time and energy devoted to the work whilst his Observatory salary was fixed the consequences could easily be seen. The Observatory work began most seriously to flag and I had to make a stand and stop this system of taking pupils... There is however a good deal to be said on Finlay's side... Finlay was about 33 Wrangler and although of course not much of a Mathematician yet he is a quick sharp fellow and there are only five Wranglers of any kind in all South Africa. Bishop Colenso, C.A. Smith, myself, Bard and Finlay".

On 9 May 1878 the Radcliffe Observer at Oxford, Robert Main, died and Stone decided to offer himself as a candidate. In writing to Airy he cited as reasons for wishing to leave the Cape:

1st. That this relaxing climate does not suit me at all. It is a fine climate for one who has no work to do, but a very trying one for anyone who has to work hard. Every hot Season I have been obliged to take tonics and my medical man has warned me that I could not long continue in this climate to work as I was now working.

2. My wife has convinced herself that the Cape, or at all events the Observatory, does not suit her. We are surrounded here by marshes and when the hot Season sets in we are liable to miasma.

3. Since the Establishment of Responsible Government at the Cape the salaries of all kinds have increased to such an extent that it is quite impossible to maintain an efficient staff here...

You can hardly expect people to live here for years amongst Colonists without adopting their ideas and Standards of salaries and living. So far as I am concerned, although we have lived in a style that the people here call mean, I have not been able to save anything worth consideration.

There were five applicants for the Oxford post, of whom Stone was by far the most senior. This, and his evident disenchantment with the Cape, must have assisted in his success (we speculate in the next Chapter on other aspects of the situation). He was informed of his appointment in December 1878 but, having made it a condition of acceptance, was allowed to remain at the Cape in order to complete work on the catalogue.

In the early part of his stay at the Cape, Stone did not enter into Cape Society as much as might have been expected. This was partly due to his somewhat controversial appointment and the unpopularity that arose from his rigid control over the Observatory. Principally, however, it was a result of Sir Thomas Maclear's continued activity. Not until Maclear became blind and unable to get around did the various niches open that Stone, as a senior scientist, might be expected to fill. He served on the Meteorological Commission from 1874, on the Council (and as an Examiner) for the University of the Cape of Good Hope from 1878 and on the Committee of the South African Public Library in 1879.

Stone's period at the Cape was remarkable for his industry in preparing the definitive catalogue of over twelve thousand southern stars and for removing some of the backlog of observations. Although Stone gathered no moss, the Observatory certainly did. At the end of March 1879 Stone wrote "My successor will find things in a great mess. I have devoted the last month to a general cleaning up which is much required, and to putting away all the books of observations and the books of reduction accumulated here during my term of office in boxes in the Record Room". His successor's comments on the "great mess" are reserved for the next Chapter. These conditions reflect not only on Stone but also on his assistants. It appears that the latter exerted themselves no more than absolutely necessary, were generally discontented and took little or no interest in the state of affairs. The fault however, must lie principally with Stone; he commanded, rather than earned, respect.

By the beginning of May 1879 Stone had completed his catalogue. He and his family sailed for England on 27 May. His Cape Catalogue of 12 441 stars was published in 1880 and earned him the Lalande medal of the Paris Academy of Sciences. At Oxford he continued to labour and produced the Radcliffe Catalogue of 6 424 stars for 1890. He died at the Radcliffe Observatory, nineteen years after his predecessor, on 9 May 1897.

5 David Gill
1879-1907

It is of significance that although the vacancy at the Radcliffe Observatory at Oxford attracted five applicants, only two (both of them unsuccessful contenders) applied for the Cape position. The Cape had few attractions; it was too well-known that the Observatory was run-down and would require much effort before it could be brought back to life. The tenacious applicants were William H.M. Christie, then Chief Assistant at the Royal Greenwich Observatory, and David Gill, previously of Dun Echt Observatory, but then unattached. Fortunately for the Cape Observatory, the best man won.

David Gill (Figure 28) was born on 12 June 1843 into an Aberdeen family of clock and watchmakers. He was educated at the Bellevue Academy and, when he was fourteen, at the Dollar Academy. While attending the latter school, he boarded with the Headmaster, Dr Lindsay, who awakened in him an interest and love of science. In 1858 he entered Marischal College, Aberdeen University, where he benefited from the excellence of the teaching staff, which included the celebrated James Clerk Maxwell, considered by many to be the Newton of the nineteenth century. Gill was inspired by Maxwell, of whom he said "his teaching influenced the whole of my future life".

Although Gill had in him "the stuff out of which senior wranglers were made" his father's requirement that he enter the family business removed all thoughts of proceeding to Cambridge. Instead, in 1860, he was taken away from Marischal and his next three years were spent in Switzerland, Coventry and Clerkenwell learning the art of watchmaking. On his return to Aberdeen in 1863 he became a partner with his father.

Throughout this time he had not lost his interest in science, and became gradually enthralled with astronomy. His profession led him to contemplate setting up a small transit instrument, from which he could supply accurate local time to Aberdeen. Armed with a letter of introduction, he travelled to Edinburgh to see his first observatory and to meet his first real astronomer - Charles Piazzi Smyth! Smyth had copied the Cape method of announcing midday with the aid of a time-gun and Time Ball. He was able to instruct his young visitor in the methods of astronomical time measurement. This was the start of a life-long friendship between the two men.

Gill set up an old Thomas Jones transit instrument at King's College, Aberdeen, and later mounted a small telescope for observations of double stars. He contributed a clock of his own make. However, he was dissatis-

28   Sir David Gill

fied with the size and quality of the telescopes, and later in 1867 he purchased a twelve-inch reflector and spent most of the year building an improved mounting. He erected it in his father's back garden. With this instrument, on 18 May 1869, he took a photograph of the Moon of such exceptional quality that the immediate acclaim changed the direction of his life. This photograph came to the attention of Lord Lindsay (later Earl of Crawford) who had for some time contemplated building an observatory on his estate at Dun Echt. Finding a young astronomer with such outstanding practical talents living only a few miles from him, Lindsay struck up a friendship and by December 1871 Gill had been offered the directorship of the proposed observatory. A quarter century later, Gill was to write "I was in business for 8 years, had married, was making £1500 a year, and working at night in my own observatory when Lord Crawford offered me £300 a year to take the direction of Dun Echt Observatory. We had no children, my wife knew where my heart lay. I had a little money with reasonable expectations of more, and in 24 hours Lord Crawford had my answer - yes. I never regretted that decision - my life became full of interest, and has so continued ever since". At this time, Gill had been married for eighteen months to Isobel Black and had taken over the running of his father's business. The opportunity was too great for Gill to turn down; he placed his prosperous business in the hands of a manager and, gently ignoring his father's protestations, he moved to Dun Echt.

During the years 1872-74, Gill and Lindsay built a well-equipped observatory. The instruments were substantial and of high quality, including, inter alia, an 8-feet Transit Circle by Troughton and Simms, a 15-inch refractor and a 4-inch heliometer. The latter device is a telescope whose lens has been sawn in half across a diameter. The two halves can be moved laterally by means of an accurately constructed screw thread. Each half of the lens forms a star image and by bringing into coincidence the images of two stars (or a star and a planet), the angular distance between them can be measured with a high degree of precision. This method was a great deal more accurate than that commonly employed of using a micrometer in the eyepiece of a telescope. However, the technique required skill and patience of a high order. Gill's practical nature soon enabled him to master the difficulties and we can date from this time the emergence of the world's greatest exponent of the heliometer.

At the same time that the Dun Echt Observatory was being built Lindsay and Gill were planning an expedition to Mauritius to observe the Transit of Venus predicted for 8 December 1874. Transits of Venus, in which the planet is seen to pass across the face of the Sun, recur in pairs (with eight years between them) at intervals of about 110 years. They had considerable significance, in that accurate timings of the instants of contact of the solar and planetary discs, made from observing sites spread over the surface of the Earth, could furnish an estimate of the distance from the Earth to Venus. From this the Astronomical Unit - the distance from the Earth to the Sun -

could be derived. In 1874 the Astronomical Unit was known only approximately: it lay between 90 million and 96 million miles.

The aspect of the Mauritius expedition that is of importance here is that Gill took with him the 4-inch heliometer from Dun Echt. He had come to the conclusion that, as first advocated by Airy, careful position measurements of the close approach of a minor planet (asteroid) could give its distance, and hence the Astronomical Unit, to greater accuracy than that furnished by the entire international effort going into observing the Transit of Venus. Lindsay took the heliometer to Mauritius on his yacht and adverse winds caused delay of a month. As a result, the intended series of observations of the minor planet Juno was severely curtailed. What results were obtained gave Gill confidence that a better planned program would give a more satisfactory answer.

The expedition to Mauritius was a modest success; Gill obtained some useful photographs of Venus as it traversed the solar disc. On the way back, Gill stayed over in Cairo at the request of the Chief of the Military Staff of the Khedive. There he measured a one kilometre baseline for the Survey of Egypt and also surveyed the Great Pyramid, measuring its height and base with an accuracy of a millimetre. Gill's abilities impressed the Survey staff and the Khedive offered him the position of Director of Surveys, but the offer was withdrawn just as Gill was seriously contemplating its acceptance. The episode was sufficient, however, to demonstrate that Gill was willing to leave Dun Echt for better prospects. Lindsay understood this situation and later accepted Gill's resignation with equanimity.

In the autumn of 1876 the Gills took up residence in London. Gill had no official position at this time but was planning a private expedition to Ascension so that he could observe the favourable approach of Mars and improve his determination of the Astronomical Unit. In London Gill came under the influence of Airy, who had known of him for some time and had visited Dun Echt shortly before the Gills left. Airy quickly realised the abilities of his young colleague and took to consulting him on matters of instrument design. For his part, Gill learned from, and modelled his outlook on, the man who had maintained the Royal Greenwich Observatory as the world's leading astronomical institution.

With the help of Airy, Gill obtained a grant of £250 from the Royal Astronomical Society and a further £250 from private subscribers (who included Lindsay and Airy) towards the cost of his expedition to Ascension. On 14 June 1877 Gill and his wife, and the Dun Echt heliometer which Gill had borrowed, sailed for Ascension. Their visit was an unqualified success; the general story can be obtained from Isobel Gill's delightful book 'Six Months in Ascension - An Unscientific Account of a Scientific Expedition' published in 1878. Gill's results from Ascension resolved the conflict over the distance to the Sun and in 1882 earned him the Gold Medal of the Royal Astronomical Society and a medal from the French Academy of Sciences. His value for the Astronomical Unit was universally adopted until superceded by his own improved measurement some years later.

On his return to England on 24 January 1878 Gill set up house in London so that he could have ready access to the Library of the Royal Astronomical Society. Samuel Smiles, the biographer, had long been a close friend [Mrs Gill's book 'Six Months in Ascension' was dedicated to him] and at his house in London the Gills met and made friends with many distinguished people. It was here that Gill was introduced to James Nasmyth, inventor of the steam-hammer and prominent amateur astronomer. Nasmyth recognised in Gill a man of his own kind - industrious, skilful with his hands, and fanatically enthusiastic about astronomy. The morning after their first meeting, without forewarning, a cheque for £1000 arrived with instructions from Nasmyth for Gill to spend it on the astronomical instrument of his choice.

In May 1878 Gill made his bid for the position of Radcliffe Observer. The Observatory possessed a magnificent heliometer (now in the Science Musuem, South Kensington) which had never been used to any purpose. Gill's reputation with such an instrument, and the galaxy of supporters (inter alia James Clerk Maxwell, William Huggins and Sir William Thomson) who gave him testimonials, should have secured him the position. Airy, who might have added his voice, declined to favour any one of the candidates: Stone had once been his Chief Assistant, William Christie was currently in that post, and Gill was equally deserving.

News of Stone's success immediately led Gill to submit his testimonials to the Admiralty in candidature for the vacancy that had opened at the Cape. Because of Stone's wish to remain at the Cape for some time, the decision on his successor was delayed and it was only on 10 February 1879 that Lindsay informed Gill of his success. Lord Lindsay had in fact been the prime mover in support of Gill's application. It nevertheless seems strange that Gill could have been victorious when the other candidate, Christie, was this time supported by Airy. Sir George Biddell Airy was recognised as the greatest living astronomer; the Admiralty looked to him for advice on all matters astronomical. One has the strong suspicion that the wily old Airy had engineered the whole sequence of changes, knowing that he himself was nearing retirement. With the Cape in a dilapidated state it required a singular personality and great instrumental competence to rebuild it. Gill was the obvious choice. The Royal Greenwich Observatory, by contrast, was in peak condition and could be handed over to any person capable of maintaining the traditions. Christie would suffice here.

At the time, however, Christie, Wrangler and Chief Assistant, was far from pleased at having lost to a man with no University degree and no position. He bore a grudge which only emerged after he suceeded Airy and which plagued Gill throughout the remainder of his time at the Cape.

Three months were left before the Gills had to sail for the Cape. Gill returned Nasmyth's cheque as no longer required; hardly had he done so when it was offered again in another context - Gill wrote to Airy on 31 March saying "I have received a very unusual and liberal offer, viz. from Mr Newall of the loan of his 25-inch Telescope for a period of years at the Cape, and of

£1000 from Mr James Nasmyth towards the cost of transporting and erecting the same". Further support was offered by the Royal Society, the British Association, and from private donors. Gill resolved to wait until he had settled in at the Cape before deciding whether to accept these generous offers, which clearly establish his eminence in British astronomy.

In preparation for his new position, Gill went on a tour of foreign observatories; he called in at Paris, Leiden, Groningen, Hamberg, Copenhagen, Helsingfors, Pulkowa and Strassburg. The impressions and friendships that he made stood him, and the Cape Observatory, in good stead for the rest of his life. In particular, it enabled Gill to visualize what would be required to develop the Cape into a leading observatory. In this, he was most influenced by the excellence of the equipment installed by Struve at the Pulkowa Observatory.

The Gills sailed for the Cape on 2 May 1879 in the R.M.S.Taymouth Castle. Before leaving they had received a long letter from Piazzi Smyth telling them of conditions at the Observatory as he remembered them from thirty-five years earlier. This letter (now in the possession of the Royal Geographical Society) warned the Gills of some of the drawbacks of life at the Observatory, but was far removed from Hendersonian melancholia.

We have dealt at some length with David Gill's astronomical experiences prior to his life at the Cape. This background is necessary to understand the changes he wrought at the Observatory. Gill's arrival in Table Bay on 25 May 1879 heralded a new lease of life: abandonment of old fashioned methods, development of new techniques and expansion of instrumentation and personnel. Under Gill the Observatory reached the peak of its existence. These achievements grew from the perfectionism, organisational ability, practical adroitness, observational experience, international friendships and, above all, determination to succeed, that Gill brought to the Cape Observatory. Unlike his predecessors, and as a tribute to the confidence vested in him, he had "no official instructions and had therefore a free hand to do that which appeared to me best for the advancement of astronomy."

When the Gills docked in Cape Town, Stone came on board to greet them. Time was short, for Stone was to sail the very next day. They drove to the Observatory and, like the Maclears four decades earlier, were dismayed at its run-down appearance, but quick to see the potential of the place. There was little for Stone to explain, other than to conduct Gill around the buildings, introduce him to the staff (Finlay, G.Maclear, the junior assistants, computers and labourers), and hand over the petty cash. The Gills returned to Cape Town and lived in a hotel for a week. Then they set up house at the Observatory and employed packing cases until their furniture could be moved in.

One of their first visitors was Miss Mary Maclear, and she took them to see Sir Thomas, blind and on his death bed, but still lively of mind. Gill's impressions of this visit have been related in Chapter 3; he undoubtedly relayed the respects of their mutual friend and advisor, Sir George Airy.

The immediate task facing Gill was one of resurrection. Before transmitting his first report to the Admiralty, he sent a letter to Airy describing the state of the Observatory. In this letter of 19 June 1879, he included several strictures which he intended to omit from his official report for fear that they would reflect badly on Stone. The following extracts illustrate the status quo:

> Mr Stone's great catalogue of 12,400 Stars is already in England, and the work is to be passed through the press by Mr Stone himself. The catalogue of 1840 is printed under Mr Stone's direction... The catalogue for 1850 I find is about half done, and, I think when we get fairly to work, I can undertake to have it ready for press in six months.
>
> No soap and water have been used to clean the Observatory for the last 9 years. During Sir T. Maclear's time the floors were occasionally scrubbed, but the shelves were never. The library cases and books were therefore loaded with dust, not having been disturbed or even dusted out for the last 15 or 20 years... The correspondence, such as there is, at present is crammed anyhow into half open boxes, covered with dust and totally without classification or arrangement of any kind... The miscellaneous Instruments - some of them very interesting and valuable, such as standard bars, pendulum apparatus, the old mural circle, a reflecting telescope, a reflecting circle, sextants, surveying apparatus, standard weights, a balance &c &c all lie huddled together on the floor of a large room [in the south east wing] .. In the Transit Circle room was all manner of things, such as the ladders of the old Mural Circle, old observing books, the desks and papers of two computers. There was more than half an inch deep of accumulated dust on the top of the Transit Piers. The Instrument itself was barked with dust and congealed oil... The old Transit Room contains half the library. Its floor was covered over with half open boxes of papers, chests of old survey work and lidless cases of ink-bottles from the stationery office their saw-dust packing strewn about the floor... None of the clocks have been cleaned for more than 10 years. Last week I... went to examine the [7-inch] Equatorial to see whether it was in adjustment... on removing a [screw] more than half a pint of water ran out of the Instrument! ...I was annoyed to find frequent notice of failure of Gun Fire, and dropping of the Time Balls at Cape Town, Port Elizabeth & Simons Bay. On endeavouring to trace the cause I found that some of our joints were made by simply twisting one wire around another... The Astronomer's room is simply uninhabitable. A good many years ago Sir Thomas Maclear imported some swarms of English Bees. Somehow the Bees selected as their nest the space under the floor of Sir Thomas' room, and there they lived and multiplied. In time however the smell of honey and dead bees became decidedly unpleasant, and attempts were made to expel them, but to no purpose. Mr Stone also tried in vain, and now the stench is overpowering, and the Bees are extending their proceedings under other

parts of the Observatory. The whole floor of the Astronomers Room at least must come up, & the Bees expelled at whatever cost. ...The photoheliograph rooms & the Carpenter Shop and stores are all in equally unsatisfactory order - and the Carpenter, a worthless drunken fellow, I have dismissed.

In a later letter to Airy, Gill added "Common decency requires that the grounds should be kept in respectable order. You can imagine their condition when I tell you that for many years nothing whatever has been done towards keeping them in order but rather the reverse. Mrs Stone kept pigs. Pigs are fond of bulbs with which the ground abounds. [One of the species of bulb was the Moraea aristata, which grows still in the Observatory grounds but nowhere else in South Africa]. The pigs were allowed to roam their own sweet wills - I leave you to imagine the condition of our lawns!!"

Finlay and the other assistants quickly came under the spell of their new Director and set to work with rejuvenated vigour. In the tradition of his predecessors, Gill found it necessary to use some of his own funds to supplement those available for repairs. The 7-inch refractor was cleaned, its pivots re-turned at Simonstown and its lens sent home for repolishing. The old 3-inch refractor was thrown out and its wooden dome repaired. The rebuilt magnetic observatory was converted into a record room. Gill would have liked to have replaced the Transit Circle with one of better design, but Airy did not agree that his design was out-moded and Gill had to settle for some improvements in the micrometers. Improvements were also made to the environs: "Surrounding the Observatory hill is a considerable extent of undrained marsh-land filled with rank rushes. These rushes I am gradually clearing away, and am planting blue-gum trees (Eucalyptus) instead. This when carried out will I believe, contribute materially to the health of the Observatory". At the end of 1879 Gill reported "a good deal of sickness among the families of the Observatory staff" and "I had previously thought of the impurity of the water, and indeed on my arrival here I was warned by several friends of the late Mr Froude...that there was no doubt Mr Froude had died from drinking bad water when on a visit to the Observatory". These comments promptly resulted in the first piped water supply to the Observatory.

The days of Fallows were still not quite over: on the 14 October 1879 Klerk's Kraal was sold for £460 and Gill requested that the funds be used for building a residence for the Fourth Assistant. The Admiralty refused. Again, a year later when Gill had started several new observational projects, he applied for additional staff and expenses, to be met with the rebuff "My Lords cannot recognise any necessity for such an expenditure, founded on the desire to complete investigations which your energy has led you to take up". One venture in which he was successful, however, was in the addition of two (later three) Kroomen (negro labourers from Simonstown

Dock Yard) to the staff. These were employed as messengers and in keeping the Observatory grounds in order. Three Kroomen that gave dedicated service were Peasoup, Saltwater and Sam Weller.

Before leaving England, Gill had decided that the fastest and surest way of filling one of the instrumental deficiencies at the Cape was to purchase the Dun Echt heliometer out of his own funds. Lindsay acquiesced and Gill, selecting only the telescope tube of the heliometer, ordered a new mounting from the firm of Sir Howard Grubb in Dublin. The beloved heliometer arrived in Cape Town at the end of December 1880 and was installed in the north-east dome vacated by the 3-inch. It was followed hotfoot on 31 January by W.L. Elkin, a young American doctoral student, whom Gill had met during his visit to Strassburg. Elkin had expressed great enthusiasm to participate with Gill in heliometer measurements of the parallaxes of stars in the southern hemisphere. From his arrival, Elkin lived as a guest of the Gill family, receiving no salary, and took an equal share of work with the heliometer. By the time he sailed for Yale Observatory on 16 May 1883, Elkin and Gill between them had measured parallaxes for nine stars, inter alia confirming the large parallax of Alpha Centauri first detected by Henderson. These results, the product of several hundred nights of laborious work, constituted the first body of parallax measurements in the southern hemisphere and were the equal of anything produced in the north.

The offer of Newall's 25-inch refractor had not been forgotten. However, Airy and other powers in England decided it would not be correct for the Admiralty to have such a large instrument merely on loan. Instead, Airy drafted a long report recommending that the Admiralty acquire such an instrument for themselves. Gill and Airy were bitterly disappointed when the Treasury turned them down. Gill determined to try again when he could better justify such an instrument.

The year 1882 marked a turning point in Gill's life, in the development of the Cape Observatory and, indeed, in the whole history of astronomy. Shortly before dawn of 8 September Finlay was returning to his house when he noticed a bright comet in the eastern sky. He returned to the Observatory and made what turned out to be the first accurate positional measurements on this, the Great Comet of 1882. The comet itself attracted world-wide attention, being visible in the daytime as it passed very near the limb of the Sun. Several photographers in Cape Town and elsewhere managed, with their ordinary portrait equipment, to obtain blurred pictures of the comet. Gill, hearing of these modest successes, and drawing on his experience with photography of the Moon and the Sun, decided to attempt some more worthwhile studies. There was little point in photographing the comet with available telescopes; it was of such large size that only a small portion could be included in their fields of view. Instead, Gill hit on the idea of mounting a portrait camera (which has a wide field of view) on the same mounting as a telescope and thus, by guiding the telescope to follow the motion of the comet across the sky, obtain unblurred images. The experiment was carried out with the aid of Mr Allis, a photographer of Mowbray who was experienced in the use of the recently invented dry plates and who contributed the camera. The result was a great success; the photographs were the finest that had ever been obtained of a comet.

The new epoch in the history of astronomy commenced when Gill saw that he had not only secured excellent comet pictures; his photographs, despite the small ($2\frac{1}{2}$ inches) aperture of the camera, had also registered the images of myriads of stars. The possibility was immediately suggested of using more powerful cameras to produce star-maps and charts to any required degree of faintness. Until that time, star charts had been constructed by painstaking plots of stars viewed through the telescope. Henceforth it would be possible to chart thousands of stars on each photographic exposure. Furthermore, these photographs could be used for accurate measurements of the positions and brightnesses of the stars. Gill promptly sent a short communication to the Paris Academy of Sciences where it was published on 26 December 1882. The effect of this announcement was that for the next half-century the work of many observatories around the world, including that at the Cape, was devoted to exploration and exploitation of Gill's discovery. Another consequence was that in June 1883 Gill was elected, belatedly according to some opinions, to Fellowship of the Royal Society.

The year 1882 included another event, of lesser importance but possessing some influence on the direction that Gill's research was to take in the years to come. On 6 December the second of the pair of Transits of Venus was due. Again an international effort was launched to observe the phenomenon. Gill sent Finlay and the Third Assistant, R.T.Pett, to erect a temporary observatory at Aberdeen Road while he and the rest of his staff prepared themselves at the Observatory. A new 6-inch refractor had been acquired for the Transit observation and Gill mounted it on the top of the old Wind Tower with a revolving dome to cover it. It was this instrument that he used as a guide telescope for his comet photographs.

The British Transit of Venus Expedition journeyed to Montague Road (now Touwsrivier) and an American party set up their instruments at Wellington. At the head of the latter was Professor Simon Newcomb, the leading theoretical astronomer in the United States and destined to succeed Airy in meridian astronomy as the theoretician par excellence. Newcomb and Gill had met in 1873 at a Congress in Hamburg when both were rising stars. Their reunion in Cape Town in 1882 was a meeting of giants. Together they planned the observational program that could most benefit Newcomb's studies. Over the years Newcomb analysed a mass of material originating from observations all over the world, but it was to Gill's heliometer measurements that he turned when he settled the final decimal place. The voluminous correspondence, both humorous and profound, between the two men continued until Newcomb's death in July 1909.

Although the Transit of Venus was well-observed the results discussed by Newcomb showed that the method possessed practical difficulties which rendered it inaccurate. Gill's value for the Astronomical Unit remained uncontested.

Improvements in the accuracy of determination of the Astronomical Unit were possible if further observations could be made of minor planets during close approaches to the Earth. Gill had noted that in 1888 and 1889 the minor planets Iris, Victoria and Sappho would make particularly favourable approaches. To observe these it would be essential to use a larger and better designed heliometer than Gill's own. Such an instrument could also be used for furthering his work on stellar parallaxes. The importance he attached to acquiring this instrument was such that Gill decided to visit England and represent it in person. During his visit in April-September 1884 he convinced the Admiralty and Treasury of his need and consequently paid a visit to Messrs Repsold in Hamburg with orders to construct the new 7-inch heliometer.

Edinburgh University were celebrating their Tercentenary in 1884 and Piazzi Smyth had been asked to name two astronomers worthy of receiving honour. He chose Gill and Newcomb; the latter was unable to attend, but Gill journeyed to Scotland and received his LL.D. honoris causa. It was his second such honour - the University of Aberdeen had conferred a similar title upon him earlier. Gill wrote to Newcomb "what kind of laws I am learned in I have yet to ascertain".

Gill had extensive discussions with William H.M. Christie, who had succeeded Airy as Astronomer Royal in September 1881. At this time any latent animosity on the part of Christie was not evident; in fact he had strongly supported Gill's request for the heliometer. Their talks included the possibility of appointing a Board of Visitors to the Cape Observatory. The Royal Greenwich Observatory had possessed such a Board since 1710; its function was to evaluate the work carried out by the Observatory and also to support the Astronomer Royal in obtaining funds for worthy projects. The Cape Observatory under Fallows had the assistance of the Board of Longitude, but after its demise in 1828 the Astronomer at the Cape had to fight his own battles. In Maclear's time, as we have seen, Sir John Herschel proved a valuable ally and later Airy took upon himself the functions of a Board of Visitors to the Cape. Gill failed to settle the point before he returned to the Cape and left the matter in Christie's hands. He, however, did nothing further, which resulted in difficulties for Gill in later years.

On Gill's return to the Cape he commenced work on the photographic survey of the southern sky. With Christie's support, he had obtained a grant of £300 from the Royal Society, part of which was to be used for a 6-inch diameter lens specially made by Dallmeyer. Dallmeyer had also loaned him a 6-inch lens to enable work to begin at once. Gill made a square wooden tube for the lens and mounted this camera in place of his heliometer tube on the Grubb mounting in the north-east dome (Figure 29). The $3\frac{1}{2}$-inch Dol-

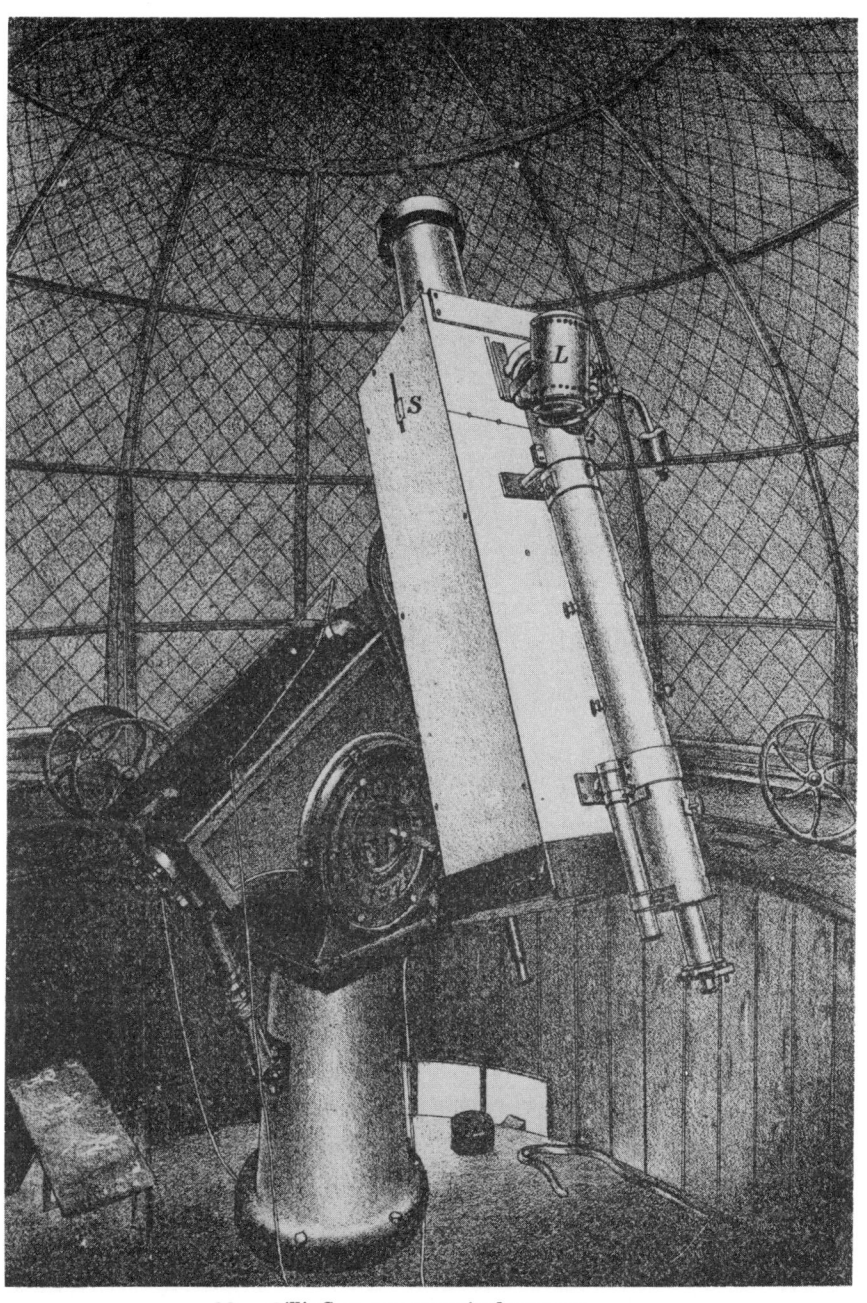

29 Gill's first astronomical camera

lond telescope which, with its mounting, had originally occupied the dome, was added as a guide telescope. Mr C.Ray Woods, who had been engaged as a photographer from England, arrived on 18 February 1885 and the first plates of the "Cape Photographic Durchmusterung"* (CPD) were taken on 15 April.

In November 1886 the new Dallmeyer lens arrived. Gill removed the first camera with its guide telescope from the mounting and installed the new camera with a guide telescope made from the lens of the old 10-feet Transit Instrument. As this instrument was too large to fit into the north-east dome, he mounted it (Figure 30, view 11) near the Wind Tower in a hut that he had originally used for his heliometer on Ascension Island in 1878. On the same mounting was fixed a 9-inch camera purchased with £200 donated by James Nasmyth.

The new camera had a smaller useful field of view than the old and Gill decided to construct the CPD solely from photographs taken with the latter. He had its lens repolished by Dallmeyer and when it returned in April 1888 it was erected on the mount of the 6-inch telescope (on the Wind Tower) which was taken temporarily out of service.

Until October 1887 the exposures were made by C.Ray Woods. After that date Henry Sawerthal was also engaged. Their combined efforts, in which over 2500 exposures were made and every piece of the southern sky was photographed twice, terminated in December 1890. Sawerthal resigned from the Observatory at this point; Woods continued as photographer until 1897 and then as a Computer until his resignation in 1901.

In following the success of the CPD we have omitted the trials that it gave to Gill. The Royal Society grant for 1885 was renewed in 1886 but in November of that year Gill was warned that no decision would be made on its continuation until after the Astrographic Congress at Paris in 1887. There were rumours that an effort was to be made to photograph the whole sky which would make the CPD redundant before it had hardly commenced.

Gill's photographs of 1882 had excited the interest of the Brothers Henry, astronomers and opticians at the Paris Observatory. They at once started work on construction of an astrographic telescope (simply a larger version of Gill's camera) and in 1886 sent some of their results to Gill. He was so impressed that he suggested that, through international collaboration, the whole sky could be photographed with such instruments and from these plates a star catalogue should be constructed. He proposed that a meeting should be convened to organise the effort. These proposals were accepted and Gill, elected President of the Congress, journeyed to Paris in April 1887. Thus was born the Carte du Ciel and Astrographic Catalogue. Until his retirement, Gill was the principal organiser in this, the largest international astronomi-

*The Northern hemisphere catalogues were the Bonner Durchmusterung prepared by Argelander at Bonn, continued as the Southern Durchmusterung by Schoenfeld to a south declination of 23°.

cal project hitherto undertaken.

The acceptance of Gill's proposals at the Astrographic Congress had an adverse effect on funding of the CPD. Christie decided that the CPD, which it will be remembered was intended as a completion of a survey that already existed in the northern hemisphere, would compete with the Astrographic Catalogue and should therefore be discontinued. Other leading astronomers disagreed. Otto Struve of the Pulkowa Observatory and A. Auwers of the Berlin Observatory intended to propose a motion at the Astrographic Congress which would strongly support the continuance of the CPD but they were forced to withdraw when Christie told them that he would withdraw his support from the Carte du Ciel if they went ahead. He also overpowered the Royal Society Grants Committee so that Gill's grant was not renewed. When the Berlin Academy of Sciences offered to supply funds for the CPD, the Admiralty, advised by Christie, declined on patriotic grounds.

It was at this point that Gill could have benefited from appeal to a Board of Visitors. He and almost all other astronomers saw the value of the CPD, not the least reason being the length of time it would take to complete the Astrographic Catalogue (in this they were correct - the final section was published only in 1962). Gill decided that the CPD was so important that he would go ahead on his own: "after thinking the matter well over, my wife and I made up our minds that we should spend our own money upon the work... We have carried out a great many domestic economies, and with a little sacrifice of capital we can manage". Henceforth Gill provided £350 per annum from his own pocket - half of his official salary.

At the beginning of the project, Professor J. C. Kapteyn, then of the Leiden Observatory, later at Groningen, offered to measure all of the photographic plates produced in the CPD. Gill accepted with gratitude and the CPD became a joint production. Together they designed a measuring machine with which the plates could be measured to high accuracy. Gill's inability to obtain funds, and the drain on his private resources, prevented him from constructing this so the work was carried out with lower precision. The final results were incorporated in three large volumes of the Annals of the Cape Observatory, which appeared in 1896, 1897 and 1900 respectively.

From 1887 until his retirement Gill had continually to fight the effects of Christie's hostility to almost every proposal that emanated from the Cape. That he was in general successful was owing to his forceful personality. The scientific community were well aware of the situation and did everything possible to aid Gill. His most valuable ally was Admiral Sir William Wharton, Hydrographer to the Navy, who like Admiral Sir Francis Beaufort in the days of Maclear, was a scientist of such eminence that he became adviser to the Lords Commissioners of the Admiralty in observatory matters.

When Gill returned from Paris to the Cape in 1887 he took with him the newly completed 7-inch heliometer. During the previous year the wooden

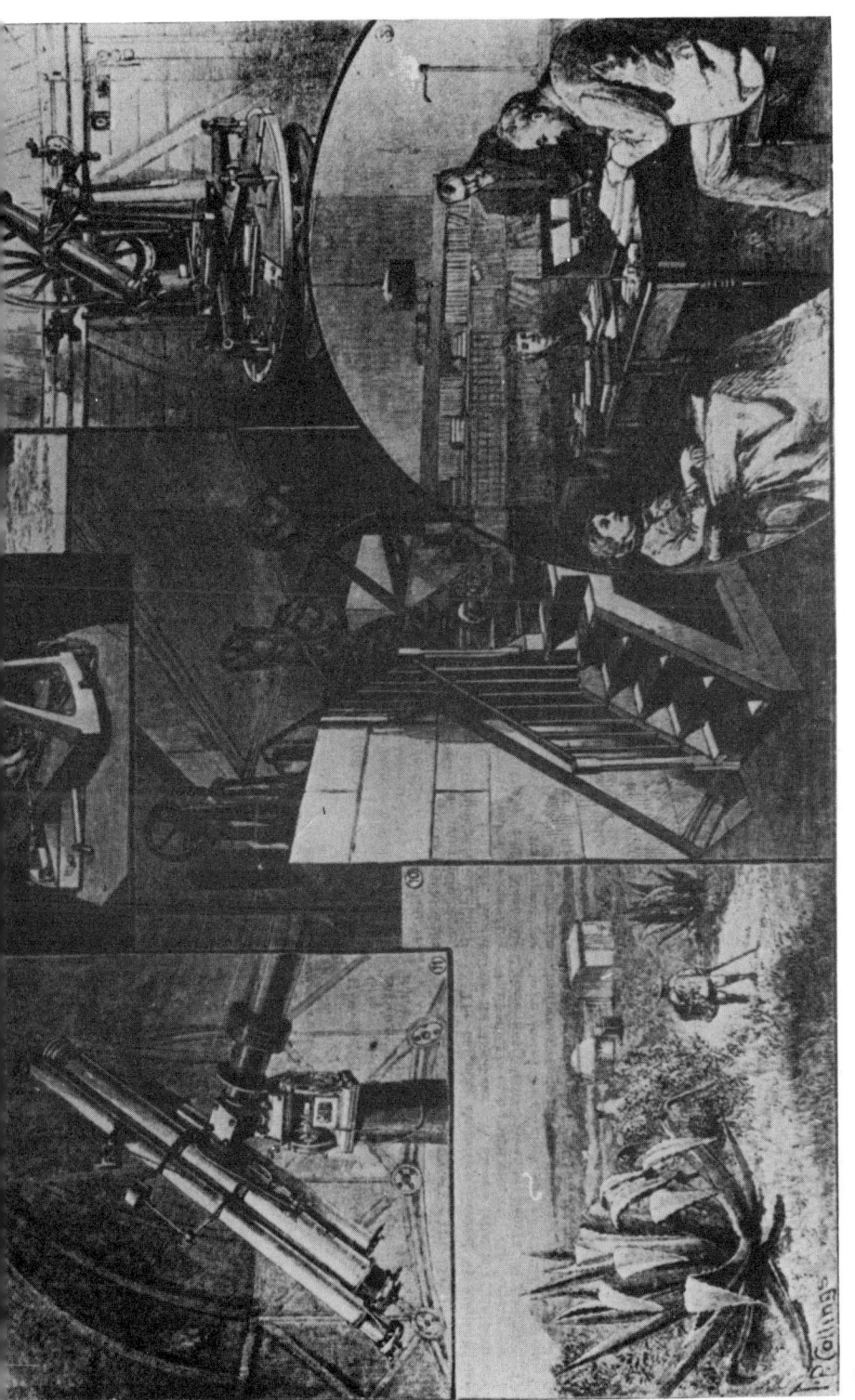

30: SKETCHES AT THE ROYAL OBSERVATORY: 1. The Devil's Peak from the Observatory. 2. The Heliometer Observatory. 3. Front. 4. The Repsold Heliometer. 5. The old wind tower and photographer's temporary dark-room. 6. The Zenith telescope or Bent Transit instrument. 7. The great Indian Theodolite. 8. The Astronomer at his desk. 9. The Transit Instrument. 10. Theodolite and Zenith Telescope huts. 11. Stellar photographic instruments.

north-east dome built by Maclear, which had housed the 4-inch heliometer, had been removed and its walls levelled. A new building, comprising a fire-proof record room and the new heliometer observatory, had been completed. The dome, an iron frame covered with papier-mache, built by Grubb was placed on brick walls which were protected from the Sun by a wooden louvre (Figure 30, view 2). By February 25, 1888 the new instrument was installed (Figure 30, view 4) and observations of stars and minor planets began.

Of Gill's work on stellar parallaxes, in which he was aided by Finlay and a visit of W. de Sitter of Groningen from 27 August 1897 to 31 December 1899, Kapteyn was later (1914) to remark "Twenty-two stars have been measured for parallax, either with the 4-inch or the 7-inch heliometer. They are the only reliable determinations of stellar parallax ever made in the Southern Hemisphere. It might almost be said that they are the first parallaxes, or at least the first extensive series of parallaxes, which command the entire confidence of astronomers... No one can study Gill's work without feeling that he has to do with the born observer, the man with the intuitive faculty of finding out every possible source of systematic error and with the unerring judgement in devising means for its removal... It cannot be doubted that by the example thus given of a perfect arrangement of the observations and their exhaustive discussion, Gill has contributed to the advancement of science quite as much and more than by the results of his observations themselves".

The observations of the minor planets Iris, Victoria and Sappho required further international collaboration. Elkin, at Yale, assisted with a heliometer which Gill had helped him to obtain. Other observatories with good heliometers, particularly those at Bamberg and Gottingen who had modelled their instruments on Gill's design, also participated. Professor Auwers came to the Cape from 24 May to 5 September 1889 to assist Gill. Twenty-two observatories made appropriate meridian observations of the planets and stars involved. The laborious reductions were carried out by Gill and his computing assistants. The latter were almost lost to him when the Admiralty, prompted by Christie, objected to their use in working on observations of a foreign origin. A direct appeal to the Lord Chancellor, who spoke to the Chancellor of the Exchequer who in turn opened the eyes of the First Lord of the Admiralty, overruled the meanness of the Admiralty.

The value of the Astronomical Unit derived by Gill was 92 876 000 miles; this was adopted as definitive for the next forty-five years. It was remarkably close to the exact value of 92 955 830 miles, deduced from modern radar observations.

A by-product of this investigation, which high-lighted its unprecedented accuracy, was the unexpected detection of periodic effects in the reduced results which indicated an error in the value assumed for the mass of the Moon. At that time, the best estimate for the Moon's mass was that deduced by U.J. le Verrier from analysis of the meridian observations made by all the leading observatories for over a century. Gill's improved value, based on heliometer observations which had occupied only a year of labour, was henceforth adopted and recognised as a triumph for the technique that Gill had championed.

At the Astrographic Congress the sky had been divided between participating observatories. The Cape was aportioned a strip 12 degrees wide running round the sky at 46 degrees southern declination. The various observatories were required to supply their own astrographic telescopes, with the proviso that all should be of the same dimensions as the one already constructed in Paris, viz a lens of 13 inches diameter and 11 feet 3 inches focal length. The instrument for the Cape was built by Sir Howard Grubb, the design incorporating ideas from both Gill and Grubb. It arrived at the Observatory on 11 June 1890 and was installed in a building completed late the previous year, situated between the Wind Tower and the "Men's Quarters" of the old magnetic observatory. The lens of the Astrographic Telescope proved faulty (which was attributed by Grubb to malicious damage by an employee after Grubb had made his final examination) and had to be returned, as also did the eye-end of its 10-inch guide telescope. They arrived back in September 1891; and, after numerous tests, regular work commenced on 26 July 1892. Between that time and Gill's retirement in 1906, over 22 000 photographs were taken with the Astrographic Telescope. These, and the ones taken at the other participating observatories, were measured with machines constructed by Repsold. The measuring engines were based on the design that Gill and Kapteyn had proposed (but had been unable to afford) for use on the CPD.

As well as the major programs on the Transit Circle, heliometer and photographic telescopes, a number of incidental investigations occupied the Observatory staff. Finlay, encouraged by his independent discovery of the Great Comet of 1882, used the 6-inch telescope to search for other comets. This telescope's elevated position on the Wind Tower (Figure 30, view 5) enabled it to reach parts of the sky not accessible to the 7-inch telescope. In September 1886 industry was rewarded and Comet Finlay was announced to the world. That same year Finlay observed and measured positions of four other comets. In February 1888 Sawerthal, while taking photographs for the CPD, also discovered a bright comet, which earned him a prize of £100 by a Mr H.H. Warner of New York.

An instrument known as the Great Indian Theodolite (Figure 30, view 7) was acquired in 1882 and used for some years in independent studies of positions of stars and for measurement of atmospheric refraction. It was constructed for the Great Trigonometrical Survey of India but, when found to be too heavy for transport to the summits of mountains, it was loaned to the Observatory. It was housed to the west of the main building in the old wooden dome removed from the north-east side (Figure 30, view 10).

A Zenith telescope (Figure 30, view 6) intended for the measurement of latitudes in a geodetic survey of South Africa, which also proved too heavy for easy use, was housed near the Theodolite in a hut (Figure 30, view 10) previously used at Montagu Road during the Transit of Venus expedition. This instrument was employed in following the small variations in latitude at the Observatory. The Zenith telescope and the Theodolite are now in the museum of the South African Trigonometric Survey at Mowbray.

A 3-inch portable Transit Instrument, used for longitude determinations at Aden, Durban and the Cape, was mounted in another of the Transit of Venus huts.

The photoheliograph, brought to the Cape by Stone, was not regularly used. In 1885 the telescope was dismounted and a coronograph was substituted. A long series of photographs was undertaken in an attempt to confirm the results obtained by Sir William Huggins who claimed to be able to photograph the solar corona outside of eclipse. The work was inconclusive.

In 1890 Gill decided that the Observatory and staff could now usefully employ a large telescope of the sort earlier offered by Newall. When tentative enquiries to the Admiralty were coolly received, he gave a public lecture in Cape Town which included an appeal for £5000. No benefactors came forward. However, in September 1894 Gill received a letter "which fairly took my breath away":

Dear Dr Gill,

It has been my wish for some time past to offer a large Telescope, equipped for Photographic and Spectroscopic work, to one of the Public Observatories in the Southern Hemisphere - and by preference to the Royal Observatory at the Cape of Good Hope.

With this object I have now arranged with Sir Howard Grubb for the construction of a Photographic Refracting Telescope of 24 inches aperture and 22 feet 5 inches focal length... Coupled with the Photographic Telescope there is to be a Visual Refracting Telescope of 18 inches aperture.

May I ask if you, as Astronomer Royal at the Cape, would be willing to accept such an Instrument, and in that case if the Official Trustees of the Observatory would be prepared to provide any assistance necessary for its efficient use?

I remain, Dear Dr Gill, Yours faithfully   Frank McClean

Frank McClean, F.R.S., after graduating as a Wrangler in the same year as E.J.Stone, had spent several years as a partner in his father's engineering firm. Since 1870, however, he had devoted his life to scientific pursuits. He built an observatory near Tunbridge Wells where he concentrated on spectroscopic observations of stars. In 1895 McClean bought one of the Astrographic telescopes from Grubb and furnished it with an objective prism (a large glass prism that is placed over the telescope lens, so producing spectra of all the stars in the field of view). After surveying all of the accessible northern stars, he brought his prism to the Cape and mounted it

31   The McClean Dome by Charles Peers

on the Astrographic telescope at the Royal Observatory. From June to October 1897 he observed those stars that could not be seen from Tunbridge Wells. In this and in his subsequent pioneering discovery of lines from the element oxygen in the spectrum of a star, McClean contributed significantly to astronomical progress. His benefactions, which included endowment of the three Isaac Newton Scholarships at Cambridge, were of long lasting value. His gift of the twin refractor (at a cost of about £10 000) gave the Cape Observatory its first major telescope and relieved the disappointment that Gill had felt after he was denied the Newall refractor.

Gill and McClean were fully occupied in 1895 with designs for the new telescope and its building. The lower, cylindrical portion of the building was erected by local contractors and the dome was constructed by Thomas Cooke and Sons; these were completed in June 1896 (Figure 31). A small building to contain electrical batteries was erected just to the north. It had originally been planned that the telescope should be installed during McClean's visit to the Cape in 1897 but this was frustrated by delays in finishing the telescope in Dublin. The instrument arrived in its packing cases on 11 April 1898. After six weeks of intensive activity it was installed in its dome and tests began. Several inadequacies were immediately evident; the mounting, of Grubb's design, was not stiff enough and the 24-inch lens performed badly. In consequence stabilizing supports had to be manufactured and the objective lens returned to Grubb for improvement. The latter was not received back at the Cape until February 1901.

To commemorate completion of the telescope an inscription stone, prepared in anticipation of conclusion in the Jubilee year of Queen Victoria, was unveiled on 10 September 1901 by the Governor, Sir Walter Hely Hutchinson. It reads "1897. The Victoria Telescope. The Gift of Frank McClean of Rusthall, Kent. David Gill, H.M.Astronomer". Although thus officially designated the "Victoria Telescope", it is commonly known as "The McClean" in honour of the donor.

The planned use of this instrument, with the aid of a fine new spectrograph, also paid for by McClean, was to determine accurate radial velocities of stars. Gill wanted by this means to provide an independent check on the Astronomical Unit by a determination of the Earth's velocity in its orbit around the Sun. This and other spectroscopic activity on the McClean telescope required the addition of a spectroscopic laboratory on the side of the dome, which was completed in July 1899.

One other major addition to the Observatory's arsenal of telescopes was made during Gill's reign. In a visit to England in 1896 he was at last able to convince the Admiralty, with the strong support of Admiral Wharton, that the old Airy Transit Circle failed to meet the requirements of contemporary meridian astronomy. The new instrument, known as the Reversible Transit Circle (RTC), was designed by Gill and marked a radical departure in the construction of such devices. The numerous innovations introduced by Gill were intended to eliminate the troublesome systematic errors inherent in earlier designs. Although criticized in its early stages, the RTC soon proved itself and later instruments have all profited from this example of Gill's genius at instrument design.

The RTC was erected 200 feet to the north-west of the main building and housed in a rectangular steel building with a semi-cylindrical roof. The whole structure was able to roll apart to leave an opening 6 feet wide. This novel design assured that the temperature of the telescope exactly matches that of the surrounding air. The building, made by Thomas Cooke and Sons, was erected by December 1900 and the telescope, constructed by Troughton and Simms, was installed in May 1901.

A great deal of attention was paid to the installation of meridian marks. With the intended accuracy of the RTC it would no longer be sufficient to construct massive stone piers whose foundations were on the surface rocks. To ensure permanence and stability it was necessary to drill down through the disintegrated upper rocks until solid rock of the stratum known as the Malmesbury beds was reached. These shafts, with a depth reaching 34 feet in one case, were lined with iron casings. (An unfortunate accident occurred at the installation of one of these linings: the Observatory carpenter and a Krooman, using an exothermic jointing compound near the base of one of the shafts, were asphixiated by fumes). At the bottom of the shaft, a long-focus lens and a reflecting trough of mercury were installed. Over the shafts, housed in brick-built huts, pillars with meridian marks observable by the RTC were constructed. The marks were adjustable so that they could be kept in position by reference (reflection) to the subterranean mercury bath. In this way movements of the RTC could be determined relative to the unmoving rock 30 feet below the surface. Great difficulty was experienced in obtaining lenses of the correct focal length; as a result the instrument did not come into operation until the end of 1905. Gill's ingeniously constructed meridian marks introduced a new era into meridian astronomy; their design has been incorporated into all subsequent developments.

Concomitant with the increase in telescope power, an expansion of the staff and additional housing for the senior assistants had been allowed. By 1905 the Observatory had been transformed from the scattering of small domes and cottages, dominated by the main building, that Gill had found in 1879. To the south and south-east were the McClean dome, the Wind Tower, various photographic telescope huts, and several houses. On the west side the RTC, numerous small instruments and all the attendant meridian marks filled a large area. The area to the north contained further residences and workshops. All were immersed in a forest of pine and eucalyptus trees planted by Mrs Maclear and successive generations of gardeners.

Even the main building had changed its profile - the unused domes were removed in July 1883 and their metal sold for scrap.

On Gill's arrival in 1879 he inherited a staff of four Assistants and three Computers. When he retired in 1907 their number had been increased to five Assistants, twelve Computers and seventeen miscellaneous clerks, measuring assistants and technical staff. During the Anglo-Boer War several staff members volunteered for military service and Observatory business was curtailed.

Several important changes occurred in the senior staff during the last years of the century. R.T.A.Innes, a Scottish-born amateur astronomer from Australia, joined as Secretary and Librarian on 1 January 1896. His zeal for astronomy led him to devote all of his spare time to assisting in a revision of the CPD and in visual discovery of double stars. His exceptional eyesight aided him in the latter pursuit and he rapidly became the leading authority in the southern hemisphere. In his work on the CPD he examined second exposures on many areas previously photographed, compared the Photographic Durchmusterung with the Astrographic work, and intercompared the Cape results where they overlapped with observations made from the northern hemisphere. As a result, many stars of variable brightness were discovered. Stars that showed detectable motions on the sky (i.e. with large "proper motions") were also found: acting on a query from Kapteyn, Innes found the star of largest known proper motion - now known as "Kapteyn's star". After the Anglo-Boer War, a Meteorological Observatory was founded in Johannesburg and, on Gill's recommendation,

Innes was appointed on 31 March 1903 as its first Director. Within a few years Innes had channeled his Observatory towards astronomical objectives and thus was founded the Union (later Republic) Observatory with its dynasty of outstanding double star observers.

On 24 October 1897 Joseph Lunt, selected for his knowledge of physics and chemistry, arrived to fill the position of Assistant detailed to further spectroscopic work with the McClean telescope and its laboratory. An early success was his discovery of the lines of silicon in the spectra of several southern stars.

Finlay retired, after twenty-five years' service, in August 1898. He had been an invaluable Chief Assistant, proving himself an expert in the use of the heliometer and devoting a great deal of his time to searches and observations of comets. His mathematical training enabled him to compute the orbits of several comets and he acted as a Mathematical examiner for the University of the Cape of Good Hope. He was President of the South African Philosophical Society from 1887 to 1889. On Finlay's retirement, Gill requested the Admiralty to provide a replacement who would be fitted for eventual promotion to Directorship of the Observatory. Their choice, S.S. Hough, arrived in October 1898 and proved satisfactory to Gill's wishes. His career will be described later.

Visitors to the Observatory included Harold Jacoby, an assistant at Columbia College Observatory, who arrived as a member of an eclipse party in January 1890. He remained at the Observatory to study the heliometer until August during which time he became attracted to Annie, daughter of G.F.W. Maclear. Their marriage and departure for Columbia resulted in the first settlement in the New World of descendants of Thomas Maclear.

An important visitor in 1903 was John Franklin Adams, an amateur astronomer and senior member of Lloyds. At his home in Wimbledon, he installed a photographic telescope by Thomas Cooke and Sons with which he commenced photography of the northern sky. In 1902 he became ill and was advised to travel to the Cape. On arrival on 28 July 1903, he was given permission by Gill to set up his telescope near the western edge of the Observatory grounds. For the next eight months he shuttled between the Observatory and the hot mineral springs at Caledon, sixty miles from Cape Town. His project completed, he returned to England where improvements in photographic emulsions and modifications to the construction of his telescope convinced him that a further trip to the Cape would be profitable. Recurrent illness prevented this and he eventually presented his photographic telescope to Innes at the Union Observatory. There (and later at an outstation at Hartebeespoort) the instrument was used to produce a fine atlas of the southern sky and it has continued in operation until the present day.

In 1905 the British Association for the Advancement of Science, a body concerned with all the sciences and engineering, met for the first time in South Africa. It is indicative of Gill's reputation that he was chosen as

Chairman of the Local Organising Committee, a task that required a visit to England of seven months in 1904 and his almost undivided attention until the end of August 1905. He greatly enjoyed the opportunity of giving hospitality at the Observatory to Professor Kapteyn, Sir William Wharton and the President of the Association Sir George Darwin. Astronomically, the highlight of the Meeting was Kapteyn's first announcement of his important discovery, based on a statistical analysis of proper motions, of the "two streams" of star motions. The acclaimed success of the Meeting was tragically marred, especially for Gill, by the illness and death at the Observatory of Wharton. In his position as Hydrographer of the Navy from 1884 to 1904, and through his friendship and admiration for Gill, he had provided the support that Gill required to raise the Observatory to its position as the peer of any in the world. Wharton is buried in the Naval cemetry at Simonstown. The Observatory possesses a memorial plaque to Wharton, made from copper taken off H.M.S.Victory.

Under Gill's directorship, the Observatory continued to determine and disseminate time. "Observatory Mean Time" was telegraphed throughout the Colony as a Noon signal. This was used to drop the Time Ball in the Cape Town Docks. A 1 o'clock signal was also transmitted, which dropped Time Balls at Simon's Bay, Port Elizabeth and East London, and which fired the signal gun on the Imhoff Battery.

However, all of the principal towns, and many of the villages, used their own local time, determined as a calculated difference from the Observatory Mean Time telegraph signals. To assure simplicity of their time-tables, the Railways used local time of the principal station on each line. As a result, each large town had at least one public clock with two sets of hands, one showing local time and the other "Railway Time". This system worked equably until the eastern extension of the railway met the western extension. At that point two different Railway Times and a local time were available! The confusion was dispersed by adoption, on 8 February 1892, of a uniform system of time throughout the Colony: that corresponding to the meridian, one and a half hours east of Greenwich. Gill had recommended that, in adherence to international policy, the meridian at an integral number of hours (two hours for the Cape Colony) should be chosen, but the Cape Parliament feared that so large an alteration would cause alarm and opted for the smaller change.

From the date of adoption of uniform time, the Observatory sent only one signal, at 10 a.m. Greenwich Mean Time (Gill insisted that his time signal should be sent on an integral hour, even though it corresponded to 11.30 a.m. local time). On 4 August 1902 the signal gun was moved from the Imhoff Battery to its present position on Signal Hill. As a result of representations from the Governments of Natal and Transvaal, who received the Observatory's telegraphed signals but for whom the Cape's time system was inappropriate, Gill's original proposal was adopted and from 3 March 1903 the whole of South

Africa has utilised the time zone two hours east of Greenwich.

The recovery and development of the Observatory, and its outstandingly succesful research program, realised the hopes that Gill carried with him to the Cape. The astronomical aspects alone would have given full occupation to a normal man, but Gill chose to live a very full life: "Soon after my arrival at the Cape in 1879 I placed before Sir Bartle Frere (then Governor) a statement of the advantages to be derived from the creation of a system of geodetic triangles, as a basis for the future accurate survey of the Colony... At last, in the end of 1882, I arranged an agreement between the Governments of the Cape Colony and Natal, for commencement of the work at their joint expense, and the field work was begun in 1883 by a party of the Royal Engineers commanded by Captain W.G. Morris R.E. and I was requested by the Cape Government to take its scientific direction... I have designed the instruments and methods employed, planned and controlled the field operations generally, and in every way in my power helped to give the work accuracy and scientific value". In 1891 Gill and Finlay participated in the measurement of the Baseline near Kimberley and the fieldwork was completed by September 1892. The results were published by Gill in 1896 as the first volume of the "Geodetic Survey of South Africa". This was only the beginning; five more volumes of the "Geodetic Survey" were to come from his hands.

In 1890 problems arose over delimitation of the boundary between British and German territory in South West Africa. Gill was sent on a mission, first to the Colonial Office in London and then to the German Foreign Office in Berlin, and succeeded in arranging a jointly financed survey. Direction of the work was again placed in Gill's hands. Field work commenced in November 1898 and was completed in 1903.

In urging a survey of South Africa, Gill had in mind more than its practical uses for land surveyors; he saw it as the first step in measurement of a grand Arc of Meridian that would stretch from the Cape to Cairo. Consequently, in 1894 he approached Cecil Rhodes for permission, and financial assistance, to push the survey to the northern limits of Rhodesia. Rhodes at first preferred that resources should be spent on more essential benefits but by 1897 he gave his assistance. At a later date Gill had some difficulty with the Administration in Rhodesia and called upon Rhodes for his support. Rhodes was sympathetic and instructed his secretary to send a telegram ordering that the money be made available. Rhodes turned to Gill and said "Fine thing, money". Gill replied "Finer thing, astronomy", to which Rhodes retorted "Too damned expensive".

After the hiatus caused by the Anglo-Boer war, Lord Milner decided to institute surveys of the two new colonies. He appointed Gill as Scientific Supervisor to his Governments of the Transvaal and Orange River Colonies. With the completion, under Gill's direction, of these surveys, geodetic triangles had been established throughout all of South Africa and northwards to within 70 miles of Lake Tanganyika, except for a gap of 140 miles between the Limpopo and Bulawayo. The British Government would not provide the funds required to close this gap: Gill, with characteristic fervour, cabled Sir George Darwin for an immediate grant of £1600 from the British Association. Darwin encountered difficulties, eventually managed to raise the funds by subscriptions from himself and various scientific societies, but required a guarantee that the survey could be completed for the amount requested. Gill cabled his reply: "Gill accepts responsibility, acts of God and the King's enemies excepted". Much of his time in the last years at the Cape was taken up in fulfilling this obligation.

The value of David Gill's contributions to surveying in South Africa is authoritatively expressed by Colonel W. Whittingdale, Director of Trigonometrical Survey, in his address at the Centenary celebration of Gill's birth: "...the story of superb achievement in the realm of fundamental Survey, which is surely without parallel in the history of Survey anywhere... He virtually assumed the position of Honorary Director of Geodetic Survey for the African sub-continent and, untramelled by Service regulations and normal administrative control, he dealt directly with governors and administrators, ordered his own equipment, appointed the staff for the work on his own terms of service, and generally got work done in a way that would be quite impossible for the most competent salaried official to do in any one of the seven different governments he had dealings with in the course of his amazing career". He added that after Gill's departure from the Cape, surveys lapsed into a "state of masterly inactivity".

There remains the task of completing the picture of Gill at the Cape with a short description of some of his non-professional activities. Unlike his predecessors, Gill has benefited from the efforts of a biographer; the reader who wishes for further information is urged to seek George Forbes's worthy book "David Gill: Man and Astronomer".

David Gill's integrity, charm and wit opened all doors at all levels of society. He was equally at home, and respected, discussing the Observatory garden with his Kroomen or matters of state with a Governor of the Colony. *
His magnetism was so great that the Observatory became, without exaggeration, the principal intellectual meeting place in South Africa. No person of distinction, be they Duke, General, Admiral, scientist, explorer, hunter or author passed through Cape Town without paying their respects and receiving hospitality at the home of the Gills. To many famous persons, Cape Town was remembered principally as "the place where David Gill lives". His regular correspondents, when they were not resident in Cape Town, included Rhodes and Rudyard Kipling.

*One Governor, whom Gill must have been particularly interested to meet, was Sir Henry Augustus Smyth, Acting Governor for eight months in 1889-90. He was Piazzi Smyth's brother. He also met Sir Henry's aide-de-camp, a nephew, Robert Stephenson Smyth Baden-Powell, who executed a water colour of the Observatory (now in the South African Library) of insufficient merit to be included here.

Gill served readily with distinction in the social positions occupied by his predecessors: he too was a Trustee of the Library and of the Museum, and an official on sundry lesser committees. He was President of the South African Philosophical Society in 1879-81, 1891-93 and again in 1901-03. During the latter period he presided over a Council of that Society whose deliberations resulted in a new Constitution with the consequent award of a Royal Charter and change of name in 1908 to the Royal Society of South Africa. In 1903 Gill was an influential founder member, and first President, of the South African Association for the Advancement of Science. He was also a founder member and first President, in 1894, of the Owl Club, a Cape Town social and entertainment club for men of distinction in science and the liberal arts.

The Gills had the happiest of marriages. Lacking any children of their own, it was their pleasure in 1892 to be able to adopt Gill's three orphaned nephews, Harry, Bruce and Fred Powell. Long before that time, however, the Gill "family" effectively embraced all members of the Observatory staff and as a result the establishment ran efficiently and happily. This was in marked contrast to the situation under Gill's predecessor.

Early in 1892 Gill was offered the Lowndean Chair of Astronomy and Geometry at the University of Cambridge; this he declined because he felt that he could more usefully serve astronomy by completing the work he had planned for the Cape Observatory. The Cambridge chair was instead taken by Gill's old friend Sir Robert Ball (until then Astronomer Royal for Ireland). Four years later Gill firmly refused a KCMG on the grounds that he did not want to join the ranks of a number of unworthy politicians who had been awarded that distinction. Instead he received a CB.

Throughout the Anglo-Boer War, Gill was consulted for his sound judgement on a wide variety of political, administrative and even military matters. The extent of his advice has never been made public but its value was recognised by the award of a KCB in 1900. (It is said that any correspondent making the error of addressing him as "Sir David Gill, KCMG" was in danger of having his letter thrown unopened into the waste paper basket).

The labours of organising the British Association meeting in 1905, and the shock of Wharton's death, broke Gill's health. This, and his wife's delicate constitution, led to medical advice that they should not risk the debilitating effects of another Cape summer. The Admiralty gave Gill permission to retire at the end of his twenty-eighth year of service: a little over a year before he would have reached the age of compulsory retirement. They also granted leave of absence, which enabled the Gills to return to England before the heat of summer, on 3 October 1906. It is curious that, unlike Maclear, Gill's name never became attached to any prominent feature in the Cape. Only "Gill's Wald" in South West Africa, remains to commemorate the man.

Retirement to Gill meant only a change in the scene of his intense activities.

He established himself in a flat at 34 De Vere Gardens, Kensington, where he could be near the activities of the principal scientific societies. He was soon called upon to be President of the Royal Astronomical Society (1909-10) and later acted as its Foreign Secretary. He served as President of the British Association in 1907 and on the Council of the Royal Society. Many smaller societies, such as the Optical Society and the Institute of Marine Engineers, also appointed him to Presidency. Numerous lectures were given, both professional and popular; the latter included the Christmas lectures to children at the Royal Institution.

Other distinctions continued to flow in. In 1908 Sir David received his second Gold Medal from the Royal Astronomical Society. He was elected the first Honorary Member of the Astronomical and Astrophysical Society of America. Foreign governments also recognised his merits: Commander de la Légion d'honneur and the German Order Pour le mérite were gratefully conferred. The highest award of the Royal Society, its Copley Medal, was to have been awarded to Gill in 1914, but this was prevented by his untimely death.

Astronomers from all countries visited Gill in London and many new friendships were established. His advice was sought on all matters astronomical and geodetical. Assistance was given to George Ellery Hale in the design of the world's largest telescope then planned: the 100-inch reflector at Mount Wilson. From 1907 until his death Sir David served as the British representative on the Bureau International des Poids et Mesures, attending several meetings in France.

The principal objective of Gill's retirement, however, was one that he barely lived long enough to satisfy: completion of his book "History and Description of the Royal Observatory, Cape of Good Hope". The bulk of the work, a description of the instruments, had been written before he left the Cape. In retirement, despite all diversions, he managed to complete the historical portion, which is primarily a retrospect of Gill's own life at the Cape. This monumental work was inspired by F.G.W.Struve's "Description de l'Observatoire Astronomique Central de Pulkova" which had strongly influenced Gill in his development of both the Dun Echt and Cape Observatories. Gill's comments on Struve's opus can as well be applied to his own: "There is inspiration to be found in nearly every page of it, for its author had the true genius and spirit of the practical astronomer - the love and precise methods of observation and the inventive mechanical and engineering capacity".

Gill's final years were not entirely taken up with business. He managed to find time for pursuing his loves of walking, shooting and golf. However, the result of getting drenched at a pheasant shoot, which aggravated a chill caught while attending the funeral of Sir Robert Ball, brought on pneumonia and complications that on 24 January 1914 terminated his life. His funeral was attended by persons of all distinction from all walks of life; Kapteyn "the dearest of all her husband's friends" was present to console Lady Gill. In accordance with his wishes, Gill was buried in the land of his birth, a grave in the grounds of St.Machar Cathedral, old Aberdeen. It is appropriate to let his final tribute be that spoken by Sir Robert Ball shortly before Gill retired:

> He is the most distinguished practical British astronomer since Bradley who has presided over one of our national observatories. As Royal Astronomer at the Cape of Good Hope, he has made discoveries more valuable than all the treasures of the Rand.

6 The twentieth century

S.S.Hough (1907-23)

H.Spencer-Jones (1923-33)

J.Jackson (1933-50)

R.H.Stoy (1950-68)

When Finlay retired in 1898, Gill's request to the Admiralty that his replacement should be of sufficient calibre (there being none on the Observatory staff) to act as Gill's own successor was favourably received. Christie was unwilling to lose any of his experienced staff from Greenwich so the Admiralty, unconsciously copying their actions in 1820, looked to St John's College, Cambridge, for an appropriate Tripos champion. Hough was their man.

Sydney Samuel Hough, born 11 June 1870, was educated at Christ's Hospital and St John's College, Cambridge. He graduated as Third Wrangler in 1892. His exceptional mathematical prowess was recognised by the award of Smith's Prize in 1894, and an Isaac Newton Studentship and Fellowship of St John's in 1895. Under the guidance of Sir George Darwin he made major contributions to the theory of periodic orbits and to the dynamical theory of tides.

Hough arrived at the Cape on 25 October 1898. Under Gill's expert tuition, his lack of experience in practical astronomy was soon remedied. His most arduous task, while Chief Assistant, was a determination of the errors of the circle divisions on the newly arrived RTC. This example of his practical ability, and his capable directorship of the Observatory during Gill's travels overseas in 1900 and 1904, gave Gill no hesitation in recommending Hough as his successor. As a result, Hough became Acting Director on Gill's departure from the Cape, and His Majesty's Astronomer the day after Gill's retirement. Hough was thus the first Astronomer at the Cape to have had any previous experience of the place.

The Observatory relinquished by Gill possessed not only admirable instruments but also a program of work sufficient to occupy it for one or two decades. The training and momentum imparted by Gill to his assistants was more than adequate for the task. Hough's was a retiring, though certainly not a weak, character. In consequence, Gill, at least in spirit, continued as Director in absentia: the orchestra, deprived of its conductor, continued to play to his implanted tempo.

The instruments that Hough took under his charge ranged from the veteran heliometer and Transit Circle to the recently operational McClean telescope and RTC. The technique developed overseas of photographic determination of stellar parallaxes was beginning to show promise, so the heliometer, a

32: Sketches at the Observatory, 1908

visual instrument, was excused from that work and used only for accurate measurements of positions of the planets. This was its sole task until it was declared obsolete in 1935. The other small equatorial telescopes received little attention until 1917 when Hough made them available to local amateurs for visual estimates of the brightness of variable stars: Messrs J.F.Skjellerup and A.W. Long became the first of a number of distinguished amateurs to make use of these facilities.

Photographic work on the Carte du Ciel was completed with the Astrographic telescope in 1906 and the instrument for many subsequent years was used only occasionally. Considerable computing was required to complete the geodetic survey of Rhodesia; this was sent to press in 1909.

The principal research programs made use of the McClean and the RTC. With the promotion of Hough a new Chief Assistant was required. This opportunity was used to provide additional support for the radial velocity program on the McClean; Dr Jacob Karl Ernst Halm of the Royal Observatory at Edinburgh was appointed and arrived on 30 June 1907. Halm hailed originally from the Strasbourg Observatory and was an experienced solar spectroscopist. With his help, Gill's project for determining the Astronomical Unit, by measurement of the variations in radial velocity of stars caused by the motion of the Earth in its orbit, was completed in May 1908; the result satisfactorily confirmed the value Gill had deduced with the heliometer. Thereafter, the McClean was used for systematic determination of radial velocities of the brightest stars in the southern hemisphere. In a discussion of these velocities in 1915, Halm added a third stream (for "Orion-type" stars) to the two streams of stellar motion announced by Kapteyn in 1905.

Fundamental positional work with the RTC, supplemented by observations made with the old Transit Circle, was continued under Hough's direction. The first fruit of the RTC was the Cape Fundamental Catalogue, published, after delay caused by the war, in 1915. In 1906-07 a classic investigation was made which involved close co-operation between the Greenwich Observatory and the Cape: a small crater (called Moesting A) close to the centre of the Moon's disc was observed nearly simultaneously from both observatories. From this triangulation an improved value for the distance to the Moon was deduced.

Only one significant change in instrumentation arose during Hough's time. In 1909 the old Dallmeyer photoheliograph, received by Stone in 1875, was sent to England for an overhaul. On its return it was mounted on the Astrographic telescope and from 1 March 1910 two photographs of the Sun were taken on every clear day; in good years the Sun was recorded on as many as 350 days. This program continued throughout the life of the Royal Observatory.

In 1911 electric light, which had been available in the domes and the main building since 1887, supplied from batteries charged by a steam-driven generator, was extended to the residences. Not until 1926 was the steam engine abandoned and the Observatory connected to a supply from the Cape Town Municipality.

The year 1913 saw publication of the first volume of the Cape Observatory's section of the Astrographic Catalogue. That same year, a series of experiments was started with the Astrographic telescope with the aim of determining more accurate magnitudes (brightnesses) of stars from photographs. This was the first foray into a new field of research that was to expand into a major program in ensuing years.

Advances in technology added a new dimension to the dissemination of time. On 1 September 1914 the Observatory supplied the first time signals to be transmitted by radio in South Africa. These comprised a short pattern of dashes, ending at 9.00 hours G.M.T., broadcast by the Slangkop radio station, and intended for use by shipping in South African coastal waters. Four years later a powerful radio receiver was constructed; time signals broadcast from other countries (France and America) were monitored and compared with the main Observatory clock.

Hough was fortunate that during the 1914-18 war his staff was only reduced by two men absent on military duty. However, printing of the Cape Annals, in which the major works of the Observatory appeared, and of the Meridian results, were delayed until after the war.

Early in 1923 Hough was taken ill and applied for sick leave; he sailed for England on 23 March. His time at the Cape had fulfilled Gill's expectations. Under his direction, meridian observations had been energetically continued, and their reduction kept up to date. The fourth and fifth volumes of the Astrographic Catalogue were published the year before his departure. Hough's early theoretical work, and his efforts under Gill, were recognised by Fellowship of the Royal Society in 1902.

A genial but shy and reserved person, Hough, played little or no part in the social life of the Cape beyond his services to a few scientific societies. He was President of the South African Philosophical Society in 1907 and became the first President when it was reconstructed as the Royal Society of South Africa in 1908. When the Cape Astronomical Association (which continues today as the Astronomical Society of Southern Africa) was founded in 1910, Hough was elected Honorary President, a position in which he served for eight years.

Hough's illness, diagnosed as cancer, did not respond to surgery and he died at Chingford on 8 July 1923. He left no descendants. His wife, a former Vice-Principal of the Good Hope Seminary at Cape Town, had fallen an early victim to the great influenza epidemic of 1918. His burial place at Chingford (10 miles north of Greenwich), not far from the disused Meridian Pillar of Airy's Transit Circle, was curiously appropriate.

The untimely death of Hough left the Observatory without a natural successor. Halm and Lunt were principally astrophysicists, not orientated towards meridian astronomy, and were nearing retirement. It was clearly necessary for the Admiralty to seek an experienced practical astronomer nearer home.

Times had changed at the Royal Greenwich Observatory; Christie had retired in 1910 and had been replaced as Astronomer Royal by Sir Frank Dyson. Dyson understood very clearly the requirements of the Cape Observatory and generously allowed his valuable Chief Assistant, Spencer Jones, to be recruited.

Harold Spencer Jones, born 29 March 1890, was educated at Latymer Upper School, Hammersmith, and Jesus College, Cambridge. Like Hough, he was a Wrangler, a Smith's Prizeman, an Isaac Newton student, and was elected to a Fellowship of his College. His evident brilliance led Dyson in 1913 to appoint him Senior Chief Assistant at Greenwich, where he remained until departing for the Cape as H.M.Astronomer at the youthful age of 33. During his ten years at Greenwich, as well as participating in the routine work of the Observatory, Spencer Jones had taken part in two eclipse expeditions. The second one, which required a journey to Christmas Island in January 1922, was clouded out; Spencer Jones made use of this unwanted holiday to write his famous textbook "General Astronomy".

He arrived at the Cape on 3 December 1923. His Chief Assistant (Halm) and three Assistants (Lunt, W.H.Cox and R.Woodgate) were all within a few years of retiring age. The programs of research initiated by Gill were nearly all completed. It was a time for revitalisation and new plans; Spencer Jones, vigorous and a natural leader, was well suited for this task.

Before he even arrived at the Cape, Spencer Jones sent instructions that photography of the entire Cape Astrographic zone should be repeated. Simultaneous measurement of the first series, taken 25 or more years earlier, with the new series would provide a mass of proper motions for southern stars. With completion of the radial velocity program, the spectrograph was removed from the McClean and henceforth it was used almost exclusively for direct photography: in particular, a large scale project for determining parallaxes of stars was started in March 1926. The RTC and old Transit Circle remained in continuous use. By the time that Spencer Jones left the Cape in 1933, proper motions of some 40 000 stars had been measured, over 13 000 parallax plates had been taken (providing parallaxes for nearly 450 stars) and nearly 100 000 meridian observations were completed. The remainder of Gill's and Hough's programs were also finished and published: a catalogue containing magnitudes of 21 000 stars in 1928 and the final volumes of the Astrographic Catalogue in 1927 (these brought the total of star positions measured in the Cape Astrographic Zone to nearly one million, contained in eleven volumes). Such a vast quantity of data, produced in the days before automation and digital computers, bears testimony to the industry of the Observatory staff and the effectiveness of their Director.

Completion of these photographic programs opened the way to another, even more ambitious, survey. In 1928 Spencer Jones began to plan a repeat of Gill's CPD, photographing the entire southern sky but to fainter limits and greater accuracy than Gill's pioneering work. After some delays, observations started in June 1931. Completion of this work (known as the Cape Photographic Catalogue: CPC) became a major objective for the Observatory over the subsequent three decades.

In June 1929 the photoheliograph was detached from the Astrographic, mounted and installed in place of the 7-inch telescope in the north-west dome. In 1937 the 7-inch was re-erected on the old photoheliograph mounting and placed on the Wind Tower.

Two special research projects were undertaken by Spencer Jones; one unexpected and the other foreseen by Gill. The first of these resulted from the discovery by Mr R. Watson, an amateur astronomer of Beaufort West, on the night of 25 May 1925, of a nova in the constellation Pictor. This bright naked-eye nova created a great deal of public interest in South Africa. Mr Watson's prompt communication of his discovery to the Observatory enabled Spencer Jones to secure a series of spectra with the McClean. His discussion of the changes in spectrum as the nova declined in brightness, published in 1931 in a monumental edition of the Annals, was hailed as a major contribution to the understanding of these exploding stars.

The other special study was yet another attack on the problem of the Astronomical Unit. In 1924 the heliometer had been used on Mars during a particularly close approach of that planet. This repetition of Gill's 1877 method proved unsatisfactory. However, in 1931 there was a very favourable opposition of the minor planet Eros for which Gill, twenty years earlier, had recommended an international effort. In 1930 Spencer Jones was appointed Chairman of the Solar Parallax Commission of the International Astronomical Union and began the immense task of co-ordinating the efforts of the 24 participating observatories. During 1931, 1153 photographs were taken with the McClean and Astrographic telescopes; these were the longest and best distributed series taken at any observatory. The task of combining and reducing the results obtained by all the participants fell to Spencer Jones. That the labour was not light may be judged from the fact that the outcome was not announced until 1942. The result was rather different from that obtained by Gill; it is no reflection on Spencer Jones's industry to report that posterity, with its advantage of precise measurements available from radar, has demonstrated Gill to have been nearer the mark.

The modern style of time signals began on 6 February 1925 with six pips, originating from the Observatory, broadcast over the radio twice daily. With this innovation, accurate time became universally available and the old Time Balls were gradually pensioned off. The first to go was that at Simonstown, dismantled 8 February 1929. The Port Elizabeth signal (actually a disc rather than a ball) followed on 30 September 1930. Finally, the Time Ball in Cape Town Docks was discontinued on 1 February 1934 and removed on 7 September that year.

No major instrumental changes were made during Spencer Jones's time. However, despite the financial stringencies of the period, he did manage in 1931 to build a new office block just to the east of the main building, on what had been the choicest part of Piazzi Smyth's garden. Three years earlier the approach road to the Observatory, which started at the Observatory railway station and belonged to the Admiralty, was handed over to Cape Town Municipality. The entrance gates, which had until that time been sited at the station, were re-erected in a new position at the south-west corner of the Observatory (the original pillars were replaced by new ones in 1954). In 1930 an entrance lodge was built, in pseudo-Old Cape Dutch style, just inside the entrance gates.

On 15 July 1926 Lunt retired after having been in charge of the McClean telescope for 30 years. (He also had to his credit the discovery of a bright comet on 18 September 1914, which was independently discovered elsewhere). As older members of staff retired, Spencer Jones promoted the lower members, many of whom had been recruited from England, and replaced them by young, enthusiastic South Africans. An exception was made when Halm retired on 7 June 1927; the new Chief Assistant was Herbert Horrocks, B.A. of St Catherine's College, Cambridge, another Isaac Newton Scholar. Spencer Jones had intended that Horrocks should be trained, as Hough under Gill, to succeed to the Directorship, but Horrocks was still too young when the change came in 1933.

Late in 1932 the Admiralty announced that Spencer Jones had been appointed to succeed Sir Frank Dyson as Astronomer Royal as from 1 March the following year. When he sailed on 10 February he took with him the respect of his many friends in South Africa: they realised that, by his work at the Cape, he had established himself as the leading British astronomer. General Smuts, perhaps consciously paraphrasing Sir Robert Ball's tribute to Gill, said that his astronomical work "is of more value than all the diamonds of Kimberley and all the gold of Johannesburg". Spencer Jones had also played a very active part in the social life of Cape Town and was held in high esteem by many citizens who understood little of his professional life.

On returning to Greenwich, Spencer Jones concentrated on working up the Eros observations. His completion of this massive work was rewarded in 1943 with a knighthood and medals from both the Royal Astronomical Society and the Royal Society (of which he had been elected a Fellow in 1930). Much of his time after 1946 was devoted to the move of the Royal Greenwich Observatory to Herstmonceux in Sussex. When he retired on 31 December 1955, that Observatory was well advanced in its reconstruction. He died on 3 November 1960.

In considering Spencer Jones's replacement at the Cape, the Admiralty consulted him in his position as Astronomer Royal-elect. It is not surprising that he agreed to release the then Chief Assistant at Greenwich: although it meant losing his right hand man at Greenwich, it would ensure that the Cape again benefited from the appointment of an experienced practical astronomer. Furthermore, Spencer Jones and John Jackson, the new appointee, were old friends and colleagues; they could expect to work in harmony.

John Jackson was born in Paisley on 11 February 1887. Educated first at Glasgow University and then at Trinity College, Cambridge, he became a Wrangler in 1910 and Smith's Prizeman in 1914. This same year he was appointed Junior Chief Assistant at the Royal Greenwich Observatory. He thus worked in close company with Spencer Jones until the latter departed in 1923. At Greenwich, Jackson had specialised in time-keeping. In collaboration with Harold Knox Shaw, the Radcliffe Observer at Oxford, he had also undertaken the enormous task of reducing the extensive observations of the first Radcliffe Observer, Thomas Hornsby. These observations, made during the years 1776-1798, were known to be of high quality but had never been analysed. The principal reason for considering them at this late date was to check the system of fundamental astronomical constants derived by Simon Newcomb. The results verified Newcomb's work.

On 27 March 1933 Jackson and his wife arrived in Cape Town. The Observatory in which they had come to live was running smoothly and had a full program of work. Jackson made no drastic changes during his directorship; rather he expanded some areas and diminished others. The heliometer was the only real casualty, in 1935 it was discontinued and its work of observing the positions of the major planets was transferred to the RTC. The 7-inch telescope replaced the heliometer on its mounting in the north-east dome. Final preparations for the publication of the proper motions in the Cape Astrographic zones took longer than expected; they finally appeared as a catalogue of 20 843 stars in 1936 and a second catalogue, of 20 554 fainter stars, in 1941. The parallax program was extended; by 1939 the one thousandth star distance had been measured. The CPC, and supporting work with the RTC, however, continued to be the most time-consuming of the general work programs.

Observations with the old Transit Circle were interrupted in 1935 when the plaster ceiling fell in: the century-old lead on the flat roof had perished in many places and rain leaked in. This section was replaced with a wooden ceiling. In 1947 the Transit Circle was taken out of use. There were no plans to install any other instruments in the main building so the chases were bricked up and the old lead roof removed. Sale of the lead furnished more than half of the cost of the new bitumen-impregnated felt roof.

The small telescopes continued to be used mostly by invited amateurs. Gill's old Grubb mounting on the Wind Tower was moved in 1935 to a square building with a run-off roof near the Astrographic Dome; it was used to carry two 5-inch aperture cameras whose photographs were used for determination of magnitudes. This program fell under the direction of Dr R.H.Stoy.

Stoy was appointed Chief Assistant on 25 October 1935 as the replacement of Horrocks, who had been invalided from service on 25 February of that year. Jackson had been on six months overseas leave from May to October 1935 and, in the absence of a Chief Assistant, Dr Halm was called back from retirement and generously acted in a temporary capacity. One other change in personnel occurred during that year - the three Kroomen, whose positions Gill had arranged over sixty years earlier and who were on the books of "H.M.S. Afrikander", were discharged and replaced by three civilian labourers.

An even older link with the past was gradually severed in the next few years. As a result of a decade of unusually low rainfall, the oldest trees in the Observatory grounds (Figure 31) died, becoming a fire hazard and a personal danger. Many of these had been planted by Mrs Maclear as seeds obtained from Sir John Herschel. From 1933 to 1937 almost all of these trees were removed and hundreds of bluegums planted in their place. In 1947 the remaining old trees were felled. At the Observatory today, it is difficult to identify any tree that might be a descendant from the Herschel era.

Unlike previous wars, the Second World War interfered seriously with the working of the Observatory. The staff were reduced to about a half: at the end of the war it was estimated that a total of 39 man-years of labour had been lost. However, the observations did not fall off proportionately; those that stayed behind served by working longer hours. Jackson changed the observing programs to concentrate on those aspects that might be lost by observatories in Europe or on ephemeral events (such as occulations and photographs of the Sun) which could not be redeemed after the war.

Publication of the Observatory's major works, normally executed by H.M.S.O. in England, was suspended during the war; by 1946 a mass of manuscripts was waiting to be published.

In 1942, "for security reasons" all domes at the Observatory were painted green. They reverted to the more practical heat-reflecting, aluminium paint in 1945.

An eclipse of the Sun on 1 October 1940 was predicted to be particularly favourable for astronomical observation. Plans had been made internationally for expeditions to the Cape, but the majority of astronomers was prevented by the war from travelling; only C.W.Allen from Australia and A.K.Pierce from Harvard eventually arrived. A planned expedition from Greenwich was abandoned, but a portable mounting was sent to the Cape and the Astrographic telescope was placed on it. All observers set up their instruments at Calvinia. Despite good weather the Observatory expedition's results were technically disappointing.

The 1940's were notable for increasing collaboration between the Cape Observatory and Universities and other observatories around South Africa.

Spectral types for all the stars in the Cape catalogues were required; assistance in this work was given by Dr G.G. Cillié at the University of Stellenbosch and by Dr J.S. Paraskevopoulos at the Boyden Observatory in Bloemfontein. Cooperation in the photographic measurement of magnitudes was provided by Dr R.O. Redman and Knox Shaw at the Radcliffe Observatory, Pretoria.* During a visit of Spencer Jones in November 1949, the only one he made after leaving the Cape in 1933, more extensive co-operation with the Radcliffe Observatory was planned. Development of photoelectric methods of measuring magnitudes, which started in 1948, was assisted by Dr R. Guelke of the University of Cape Town. Both the 7-inch and McClean telescopes were used for this photoelectric photometry.

John Jackson retired on 31 July 1950 and returned to England where he made his home at Ewell, Surrey. The Observatory that he ceded to his successor was still actively engaged in long-term programs. Under his directorship, some 1 600 stellar parallaxes had been published; the photographic work for the CPC was nearly complete, measurement of this was half finished and the first two volumes were prepared for press; the magnitude program was being pursued at an incredible rate - some 150 000 images per year.

Jackson's work was mostly of a routine nature, he made no great discoveries nor did he introduce any striking new techniques. His competence was recognised in 1938 by election to Fellowship of the Royal Society. He was awarded the Gold Medal of the Royal Astronomical Society in 1952 and served as President of that Society from 1953 to 1955. On his retirement from the Cape in 1950 he was made a CBE. After a brief illness he died on 9 December 1958.

On 1 August 1950 the Chief Assistant, R.H. Stoy, was promoted to replace Jackson. The Observatory at that time had a large program of work and every expectation of an assured future; Stoy would have been incredulous if anyone had intimated that he was destined to be the last of H.M. Astronomers at the Cape.

Richard Hugh Stoy was born 31 January 1910 at Wolverhampton, Staffordshire and educated at the local Grammar School and at Gonville and Caius College, Cambridge. From Cambridge, in 1933, he travelled on a Commonwealth Fund Fellowship to the Lick Observatory, California, where he studied the spectra of planetary nebulae. His appointment as Chief Assistant to Jackson brought him to the Cape in 1935. As we have already noted, Stoy's principal work under Jackson was the development of techniques of stellar photometry, and application of these to the measurement of the large numbers of magnitudes required for the CPC. A subsidiary program was the establishment of a number of accurately measured magnitudes that could be used as reliable standards.

*Jackson's old colleague, H. Knox Shaw, the Radcliffe Observer, had been the principal instigator in the move of the Radcliffe Observatory from Oxford to Pretoria. Installation of its new telescope, a 74-inch reflector, was interrupted by the war.

As H.M.Astronomer, Stoy's first obligation was to finish the work initiated by Spencer Jones. Completion of the CPC required only routine toil. The supplementary program on the RTC was suspended in 1950, while it was modernised; at its conclusion in 1951, Stoy wrote in his report "Thanks to Gill's genius, this instrument still remains one of the finest in the world". In its improved form it was used just as energetically as in Hough's day: in 1956, for example, 11 801 transits were observed. It was further modernised in 1960.

In contrast, the old Transit Circle had not been used for several years and was not considered worthy of redemption. It was dismounted in 1950 and sold as scrap metal. Its massive piers were removed in the following year: henceforth the Circle room became an extension to the library and no observational instruments were left in the main building. The building itself had stood for over 120 years: a continuing tribute to the standards demanded by John Skirrow. Nevertheless, the interior was troubled by dampness and to rectify this, in 1953 the exterior was stripped and replastered. The old wooden lantern over the centre room was leaky and a potential disaster in strong winds; in 1961 it was demolished and replaced by a glass skylight.

The McClean telescope continued to alternate in use between photoelectric photometry and parallax determinations. It had received such extensive service that by 1952 new bearings were required. (Earlier, in 1946, it was found that the wheels of the McClean dome had worn a deep groove in the rail along which they run; this was cured by replacing the wheels by others with a wider rim).

Of the small telescopes, only the 7-inch was still used professionally, viz. that part of its time devoted to photoelectric photometry. They were, however, still being put to good use by amateurs. Notable among these were W.P.Hirst, who observed double stars, and R.P.de Kock, who made visual estimates of the brightness of long period variable stars. De Kock was taken on to the staff of the Observatory as a computer in 1950; by June 1958, in the twenty-eighth year of his labour of love, he had recorded his one hundred thousandth observation.

In April 1951 an agreement was signed between the Admiralty and the Radcliffe Trustees whereby one third of the time at the Radcliffe Observatory in Pretoria was made available for use by the Cape Observatory. Administration of this extra observing time fell logically to Dr David S.Evans who was appointed to the vacant Chief Assistantship on 13 March 1951. D.S. Evans had been on the staff of the Radcliffe Observatory since 1946, having arrived there from Cambridge University via a position at the University of Oxford Observatory. From the time of the new agreement, there were in general two staff members of the Cape Observatory stationed in Pretoria. Their main task was an extension of the radial velocity measurements to stars fainter than could be observed in the earlier McClean program.

As Stoy had been engaged in the determination of stellar magnitudes since his arrival at the Cape, it was natural that he should expand this aspect of the Observatory's work when he assumed the Directorship. In the early 1950's it became evident that magnitudes could no longer be properly measured with refracting telescopes. An order was therefore placed with Messrs Cox, Hargreaves and Thomson in England for an 18-inch reflector. When this arrived in 1954 it replaced the 7-inch on the old heliometer mounting; the 7-inch was fixed on the side of the new telescope to act as a guide instrument. The following year its Repsold mounting, dating back to 1886, was largely rebuilt. The shutter opening of the dome was too narrow for the new instrument; new shutters were added after the dome had been modified. The 18-inch itself did not come into routine use for magnitude determinations until early 1957.

Several other new instruments were acquired in the decade 1955-1964. As a contribution to the International Geophysical Year, the Observatory agreed to operate a Lyot Heliograph. This instrument was designed automatically to take photographs of the Sun every minute (or more frequently at times of great solar activity) in the light of hydrogen alpha. A building was erected to the north of the McClean battery house and the heliograph commenced operation in March 1958. In 1959 it ran for a total of 1400 hours and on its films 849 solar flares were detected.

In January 1958 the Admiralty signed a contract with Sir Howard Grubb, Parsons and Co. for the construction of a 40-inch reflector. Erection of the building to house this instrument, sited roughly midway between the north-east and north-west domes, to the north of the main building, was started in April 1959 and was completed a year later. The framework for the dome came from the 36-inch Yapp reflector at Greenwich, which had been moved to its new dome at Herstmonceux. After some delay, the new 40-inch telescope arrived in mid-September, 1963, and was in operation two months later. At its formal opening by the British Ambassador, Sir Hugh Stephenson, on 1 May 1964, the instrument was named the Elizabeth Telescope as a tribute to the approval "in principle" received in 1953, the year of Queen Elizabeth's coronation.

Another reflector was acquired in 1961 when Dr W.H.Steavenson, a prominent British amateur astronomer, presented his 30-inch telescope and dome framework to the Observatory. The building for it was erected near the McClean. Both reflectors were utilized primarily for photoelectric photometry.

During 1962 another structure, with a run-off roof, was constructed between the main building and the north-east dome. This housed a Multiple Refractor Mounting (MRM) on which the various cameras, until then attached to the Astrographic and McClean telescopes, could be mounted. The building also provided rooms specially designed to accommodate some of the instruments required for measurement of photographic plates.

Until 1963 the Chief Assistant resided, as had been the tradition for 135 years, in the East Wing. In April of that year, however, he moved to a house newly completed near to the western side of the main building. The East Wing was thereby released entirely for offices.

Amid all these increases to the stock of structures at the Observatory there was one deplorable loss. In the early 1950's the 6-inch telescope on the Wind Tower was still in use for visitors, but by 1954 it fell into disuse and the Tower and its dome were deemed unworthy to receive a better instrument. The cost of renovating this old building could not be justified in terms of its small potential use; it was demolished in 1966. It is sad that this unique structure, a rare example of the architectural aspirations of the 1840's, could not have been preserved for posterity.

Under Stoy's directorship the Observatory extended its collaboration with other institutions and the general public. Regularly organised visitors' nights were introduced in 1950, whereby the public could tour the Observatory and view celestial scenes through the telescopes. From about the same time, students from the University of Cape Town were employed during the long vacation. By 1955 there were usually UCT students and a lecturer from its Physics Department making use of the facilities at the Observatory. In recognition of the part played by Stoy in stimulating this development, UCT appointed him Honorary Professor of Astronomy in 1956. A decade later, Stoy was the moving force behind the University's decision to start a separate Department of Astronomy. (As a tribute to his generous aid and to his other contributions to astronomy in South Africa, UCT in 1976 awarded Stoy a D.Sc., honoris causa).

From April 1957, it was arranged that a member of staff of the Royal Greenwich Observatory would be seconded to work at the Radcliffe and Cape Observatories, thus tieing the three observatories closer together. On 1 April 1960, as a result of recommendations by H.M.A. and the Astronomer Royal, the Cape Observatory was taken under the wing of the Royal Greenwich Observatory, becoming to a large extent a southern extension of the RGO. From that time the Cape Observatory was formally under the charge of the Astronomer Royal, Spencer Jones's successor, Sir Richard van der riet Woolley, and the two observatories published a joint annual report. Finally, on 1 April 1965, the Science Research Council (previously the Department for Scientific and Industrial Research) in Britain took over responsibility from the Admiralty for running the three Royal Observatories (Greenwich, Edinburgh and the Cape). The Cape Observatory was then more fully incorporated into the RGO and temporary exchanges of staff became more frequent.

During the 1960's the quality of the Observatory as an astronomical observatory site began to deteriorate. In 1960 the Liesbeek River was canalised along the western boundary of the Observatory and a major road built by its side. The street lights it introduced were greatly augmented in 1962 by the introduction of floodlit football in the nearby Western Province stadium and by lights from a new motorway on the eastern boundary of the Observatory. (For the latter road, the Black (or Salt) River was canalised, which had the advantage of completely draining the marshes on the east side of the Observatory. The original bed of the Black River is still evident).

The greatly brightened sky made it impossible to observe faint objects. As a result, serious attention was given to possible transfer of the principal instruments to a new site, well removed from city lights. A promising site was found near to Sutherland, in the western Karroo, at a road distance of 230 miles from Cape Town. Systematic observations at the site with a small telescope began in 1967 and it was soon found to be astronomically suitable.

Concurrent with these developments, the Science Research Council had under consideration the future of the Cape Observatory, including the possibility that it may have reached the end of its useful life. The Observatory had over the years, survived several attempts on its life. As early as 1828, when the Observatory had barely drawn first breath, a letter to Davies Gilbert reported that "Some doubt is entertained by some Members of the Government, whether it is necessary to incur the expense of two Observatories, one at the Cape, and another at New South Wales". The matter was referred by the Royal Society to the Royal Astronomical Society who replied that removal of the Cape Observatory was regarded "as precluded, by its very advantageous situation on the same meridian with the principal observatories of Europe". Discussion thereafter was confined to the advisability of discontinuing the Paramatta Observatory; it was retained.

A second attack was made in 1850. The London Times for 9 April carried the report of a debate in Parliament during which "Mr Hume wished to know, what advantage was derived to science, from the keeping of the Observatory at the Cape of Good Hope; for which there was a charge of £1849 [annually]?" Airy and Herschel came to the rescue and Airy requested Maclear in future to provide an annual report so that the Observatory's work would be more readily evident to the Home Government.

In 1911 and again in 1921 there were some anxious moments. In the latter case, Sir Joseph Larmor, an eminent Cambridge mathematical physicist (and old friend of Gill), wrote to the Times protesting against a rumour that the Admiralty had plans to transfer the administration and finance of the Observatory to the Union Government. He regarded the possibility of cutting the strong ties between the Greenwich and Cape observatories as fatal to the latter. Whether or not his fears were justified, or whether his prompt support was persuasive, is not known, but no changes were made.

By 1968, however, the emphasis in British optical astronomy had changed to the point where support was only readily obtainable for astrophysical research in avant-garde subjects. The Cape Observatory, with its accumulation of modest-sized and specialised telescopes, was compared unfavourably with the more glamorous equipage of other southern hemisphere observatories which were under construction. Little regard seemed to be given to the special advantages of a government observatory, which, inter alia, include the ability to undertake large programs that require a decade or more of sustained effort.

The insecurity generated by lack of appreciation and rumours that the Cape Observatory would be discontinued, led to the resignation of both the Chief Assistant and H.M.A. On 4 October 1968 D.S. Evans resigned and took up a new post as Professor of Astronomy at the University of Texas. On 20 November Stoy sailed from the Cape to become Deputy Director of the Royal Observatory, Edinburgh and an Honorary Professor at the University of Edinburgh.

In his 33 years at the Observatory, Stoy saw the completion of all the major programs. The first volume of the CPC was published in 1954 and the final one before his departure in 1968. The results from the RTC appeared shortly afterwards in the final issue of the Cape Annals: Volume XXII. For probably the first time in the history of the Observatory all reductions were up to date. There were of course several new programs under way, but none so major that they could not be terminated without serious loss. Stoy could be content that, in regard to research matters, the Observatory was left in ship-shape order, capable of being scrapped or re-floated according to vagaries or necessity. Stoy's contributions to the success of the Observatory were recognised in 1957 by the award of a CBE and in 1965 by award of the Gill Medal of the Astronomical Society of Southern Africa. He also received the rare honour of a special retirement conference, held at the Royal Greenwich Observatory in April 1975.

The interregnum caused by Stoy's departure was filled by the appointment of George A. Harding as Officer-in-Charge of the Observatory. Harding, who was on the staff at Greenwich, had previously been seconded to the Radcliffe Observatory and was familiar with the working of the Cape Observatory. Details of the deliberations in high places, and the pros and cons that were considered, in relation to continuance of the Observatory, are not in the public domain. It is fairly evident, however, that without the intervention of another body, the SRC would have disbanded the Observatory.

On 23 September 1970 the following statement was made jointly by the SRC in Britain and the Council for Scientific and Industrial Research in South Africa:

> Agreement in principle has been reached between the Science Research Council and the South African Council for Scientific and Industrial Research, on a joint astronomical venture covering a minimum period of 15 years.
>
> The project involves the creation of a new observing station pooling the resources, as far as both manpower and equipment are concerned, of the long established Royal Observatory at the Cape and the Republic Observatory in Johannesburg, both of which are unsuitable for further development as observing sites because of their situation in large cities. A site has been selected in the Karroo near Sutherland. This new observing station together with an astronomical base at the present Cape Observatory will be known as the South African Astronomical Observatory which will be operated as an institute of the CSIR. It is planned to come into operation

from the 1st January 1972. There will be an Advisory Committee comprising representatives of the SRC and CSIR.

Sir Richard Woolley, OBE, FRS, who will retire from the position of Astronomer Royal at the end of 1971, has accepted an invitation from the CSIR to be the first Director of the new Observatory. Sir Richard first came to South Africa as a boy and took his first degree at the University of Cape Town.

With the superior conditions to be found in the Karroo and with the pooling of resources, it is the intention to build up an astronomical facility which can make a major contribution to astronomy in the Southern Hemisphere.

Thus the life of the Royal Observatory, Cape of Good Hope, came to an end on 31 December 1971. The next day, reincarnated as the South African Astronomical Observatory, its life began anew. The history of this new institution is still being made and we must leave for posterity to describe and evaluate the changes that have or will be made. With roots extending back over 150 years, the new Observatory is growing in firm grounds; its fruits will be those of experience as well as innovation.

Further reading

Airy, W. (Ed.), 'Autobiography of Sir George Biddell Airy', Cambridge University Press, 1896.
Anon., 'The Royal Observatory', Cape Illustrated Magazine, $\underline{7}$, 97, 1896.
Bradlow, F., 'Thomas Bowler: His Life and Work', Balkema, 1967.
Buttman, G., 'The Shadow of the Telescope', Scribners, New York, 1970.
Cameron-Swan, D., 'The Rev. Fearon Fallows', Journ. Astr. Soc. S. Af., $\underline{3}$, 1, 1931.
Evans, D.S., 'The Astronomical Work of Sir John Herschel at the Cape', Quart. Bull. S. Af. Library, $\underline{12}$, 44, 1957.
Evans, D.S., 'Dashing and Dutiful', Science, $\underline{127}$, 935, 1958.
Evans, D.S., 'Historical Notes on Astronomy in South Africa', Vistas in Astronomy, $\underline{9}$, 265, 1967.
Evans, D.S., Deeming, T.J., Evans, B.H. and Goldfarb, S., 'Herschel at the Cape', Balkema, Cape Town, 1969.
Fernie, D., 'The Whisper and the Vision', Clarke, Irwin and Co., Toronto, 1976.
Forbes, G., 'David Gill, Man and Astronomer', Murray, London, 1916.
Gill, I., 'Six Months in Ascension', Murray, London, 1878.
Gill, D., 'A History and Description of The Royal Observatory', Cape of Good Hope, H.M.S.O., 1913.
Hurly, R.F., 'Fallows' Observatories', S. Af. Survey Journ., $\underline{16}$, 63, 1977.
Laing, J.D. (Ed.), 'The Royal Observatory at the Cape of Good Hope, 1820-1970', Publ. by the Roy. Obs., 1970.
Lewcock, R., 'Early Nineteenth Century Architecture in South Africa', Balkema, Cape Town, 1963.
McIntyre, D., 'An Astronomical Bi-Centenary: The Abbe de la Caille's visit to the Cape 1751-1753', Quart. Bull. S. Af. Library, 5, March 1951.
Moore, P. and Collins, P., 'The Astronomy of Southern Africa', Hall, London, 1977.
Warner, B., 'Astronomical Archives in Southern Africa', Journ. Hist. Astr. $\underline{8}$, 217, 1977.
Warner, B., 'The Herschel Obelisk', Quart. Bull. S. Af. Library, $\underline{32}$, 56, 1978.

Warner, B., 'Early Years of the Magnetic Observatory', S. Af. Journ. Sci., 74, 82, 1978.

Warner, B., 'Charles Piazzi Smyth: Pioneer Cape Photographer', Africana Notes and News, 23, 52, 1978.

The Monthly Notices of the Astronomical Society of Southern Africa have, over the years, contained many historical articles about the Royal Observatory.

Appendix

Principal Staff of the Royal Observatory

Astronomers Royal/H. Majesty's Astronomers at the Cape

Fearon Fallows	1820 - 1831
Thomas Henderson	1831 - 1833
Thomas Maclear	1833 - 1870
Edward James Stone	1870 - 1879
David Gill	1879 - 1907
Sydney Samuel Hough	1907 - 1923
Harold Spencer Jones	1923 - 1933
John Jackson	1933 - 1950
Richard Hugh Stoy	1950 - 1968

First Assistants/Chief Assistants

James Fayrer	1820 - 1822
Patrick Scully	1822 - 1824
William Ronald	1824 - 1831
William Meadows	1831 - 1834
Charles Piazzi Smyth	1835 - 1845
William Mann	1846 - 1872
William Henry Finlay	1873 - 1898
Sydney Samuel Hough	1898 - 1907
Jacob Karl Ernst Halm	1907 - 1927
Herbert Horrocks	1927 - 1935
Richard Hugh Stoy	1935 - 1950
David Stanley Evans	1951 - 1968

Officers-in-Charge (other than during temporary absences of H.M.A.)

John Fry	1831 - 1832
William Meadows	1833
Jacob Karl Ernst Halm	1923
George Alfred Harding	1968 - 1971

In addition to these senior officers, about 250 others have served at the Observatory. It is pertinent to note that many spent almost their entire working lives in the congenial employ of the Observatory; we select for illustration:

G.W.H.Maclear, 1852-1893; R.T.Pett, 1876-1919; J.A.J.Pead, 1890-1923; W.H.Cox, 1883-1925; R.Woodgate, 1890-1928; R.W.Cheeseman, 1900-1932; A.H.Pilling, 1903-1937; T.R.Miller, 1898-1937; A.J.Wilkin, 1902-1938; H.F.Mullis, 1901-1944; J.W.Jackson, 1903-1946; J.H.Pierce, 1911-1950; M.E.Coates, 1902-1950; L.T.Davis, 1920-1957; J.B.G.Turner, 1925-1957; F.J.Driver, 1924-1957; E.H.Tibbits, 1923-1961; A.Menzies, 1923-1967; T.W.Russo, 1930-1971*; J.v.B.Lourens, 1933-1969.

*Continued in service with S.A.A.O.

Index

Airy, Sir George 6,30,31,46,49
  54,56,60,61,65,70,71,73,74,
  75,77,83,84,86,87,88,89,90,
  100,113,123,129
Anglo-Boer War 101,104,106
Arc of Meridian 50,51,56,57,69,
  70,104
Ascension 83,92
Astrographic Catalogue 92,93,101,
  113,114
Astrographic Telescope 97,99,112,
  113,115,118,121
Astronomical Unit 82,83,90,96,115
Auwers, A. 93,96
Baden-Powell, Robert S.S. 105
Baily, Francis 46,55
Ball, Sir Robert 106,107,108,116
Banks, Sir Joseph 1
Barrow, Sir John 1,10,11,13
Bathurst, Earl of 1,23
Beaufort, Sir Francis 32,39,55,56,
  93
Bell, John 23
Bessel, W. 36
Bestandig, Carel 7
Bird, Col. 7,8,9
Board of Longitude 1,2,3,5,25
Bootle, Sarah 6,12
Bourke, Sir Richard 23,29
Bowler, Thomas 40,41,44,45,49,
  63,71,129
Bradley, James 56,108
Brenton, Sir Jahleel 6
Calton Hill Observatory 32,36
Campbell, Admiral Patrick 47
Cannon, John 16,18,19
Cape Photographic Durchmusterung
  (CPD) 92,93,97,101,115
Cape Town Waterworks 6,23
Challenger, H.M.S. 76
Childe, Revd George 62
Christie, Sir William H.M. 80,84,
  90,93,96,109,114
Cole, Sir Lowry 23
Comets 53,58,88,89,97,102,116

Constable, John 32
Cooke, Thomas and Sons 99,100,102
Cooper, Sir Astley 37
Darwin, Sir George 103,105,109
De Kock, R.P. 120
De Sitter, W. 96
Dollond, George 2,25,63,91,92
Donkin, Sir Rufane 6,8,9,10,13
Dun Echt Observatory 80,82,83,88
D'Urban, Sir Benjamin 40
Dyson, Sir Frank 114,116
Eardley-Wilmot, Lieutenant Frederick 59,61
Elkin, W.L. 88,96
Evans, David S. 120,124,127,129
Everest, Colonel George 50
Fallows, Fearon Chapter 1 passim,
  31,35,36,40,44,46,50,53,56,59,
  65,66,70,87,90,127,129
Fallows, John 3
Fallows, Mary Anne (nee Hervey) 5,
  8,12,16,23,27,28,29,30,39
Fayrer, James 6,7,8,12,13,22,29,
  44,49,127
Feldhausen 44,45,55
Finlay, William H. 75,77,85,87,88,
  89,96,97,102,104,109,127
Forbes, George 105
Frere, Sir Bartle 104
Fry, Revd John 30,31,127
Garden Rozenhof 9
Garden Zorg en Lust 9,15
Geodetic Survey 104,112
Gibbs, Joseph 52,57
Gilbert, Davies 1,40,123
Gill, Sir David Chapter 5 passim,71,
  109,112,113,114,115,116,117,118,
  120,123,127,129
Gill, Isobel 82,83
Great Indian Theodolite 97
Grubb, Sir Howard 88,96,97,98,99,
  117,121
Guelke, Dr R. 119
Hale, George E. 107
Halm, Jacob K.E. 112,113,114,116,
  118,127

Harding, George K. 124,127
Heliometer 82,83,88,89,90,93,96,
  97,102,109,110,112,115,117
Henderson, Captain Alexander 57
Henderson, Thomas Chapter 2 passim,
  37,39,44,46,49,60,62,88,127
Hely Hutchinson, Sir Walter 100
Herschel, Sir John F.W. 1,4,5,6,
  7,10,14,34,39,40,41,44,45,46,
  47,49,50,51,53,54,55,56,58,
  59,60,62,63,65,69,70,71,74,77,
  90,118,123,129
Herschel, Julia 77
Herschel, Sir William 4,25,39,40,74
Hervey, Revd H.A. 3,4,12
Hirst, W.P. 120
Horrocks, Herbert 116,117,127
Hough, Revd George 28
Hough, S.S. 102,109,112-114,116,
  120,127
Huggins, Sir William 84,98
Innes, R.T.A. 101,102
Ingram, J. 20
Jackson, John 117-119,127
Jacoby, Harold 102
Johnson, Manuel J. 23,25,36,73
Jones, Thomas 2,56,63,80
Kapteyn, J.C. 93,96,97,101,103,
  107,112
Kipling, Rudyard 105
Klerk's Kraal 22,47,87
Klipfontein 50,52,57,76
Knox-Shaw, Harold 117,119
Lacaille, Abbe Nicholas L. 2,50,
  51,52,56,57,69,76,129
Larmor, Sir Joseph 123
Lee, Dr John 41,44,45
Le Verrier, V.J. 96
Lewcock, R. 6,18,129
Liesbeek River 11,15,27,59,61,122
Lindsay, Lord 82,83,84
Livingstone, David 70
Long, A.W. 112
Lunt, Joseph 102,113,114,116
Maclear, George W.H. 62,74,75,77,
  85,102,128
Maclear, Commander John F.L.P.
  76,77
Maclear, Mrs. Mary 34,37,39,40,
  41,44,61,70,101,118
Maclear, Miss Mary 34,61,71,85
Maclear, Sir Thomas Chapter 3 passim,22,30,34,73,74,75,76,77,78,
  85,86,90,96,102,106,123,127
Magnetic Observatory 59,60,97,129

Magrath, Sir George 37
Magrath, Dr T. 37
Main, Revd Robert 73,77
Mann, General Cornelius 55
Mann, William 55,56,58,61,62,65,
  66,70,74,75,127
Mauritius 82,83
Maxwell, J.C. 80,84
McClean, Frank 98,99,100
McClean (Victoria) Telescope 100,
  101,102,109,112,114,115,119,
  120,121
Meadows, Lt William 31,32,34,35,
  39,41,49,127
Milner, Lord 104
Moller, Heinrich P. 9
Moraea Aristata 87
Morris, Capt R.E. 104
Morton, Pierce 60
Mostert, Cornelis 12,15
Mural Circle 2,16,20,21,23,25,27,
  28,29,30,32,36,45,50,55,56,63,
  65,66,69,86
Nasmyth, James 84,85,92
Newcomb, Simon 89,90,117
Paramatta Observatory 23,123
Pearse, Theed 37
Pearson, Dr William 1,5
Pennell, William 15
Pett, R.T. 89,128
Photoheliograph 77,98,112,115,121
Piazzi, Guiseppe 39
Pond, John 2,20,47,56
Radcliffe Observatory 79,80,84,119,
  120,122,124
Radcliffe Observer 25,73,77,84,
  117,119
Rennie, John 5,6,17,18
Reversible Transit Circle (RTC)
  100,101,109,112,114,117,120,
  121,124
Rhodes, Cecil 104
Richards, Captain G.H. 71
Richardson, William 31
Ronald, Capt William 20,21,22,23,
  25,27,28,31,35,49,127
Ross, James Clark 59
Royal Astronomical Society 1,23,
  25,30,39,60,74,83,84,107,116,
  119,123
Royal Greenwich Observatory 2,5,
  30,31,47,56,57,58,65,73,75,
  80,83,84,90,109,112,114,116,
  117,118,121,122,123,124

Royal Society 1,10,28,39,40,70,74, 85,89,90,92,93,107,113,116,119, 123
Royal Society of South Africa 106, 113
Sabine, General Edward 59
St George's Church 14,23,28
St Helena 23,36
Salt (Brak) River 11,15,27,47,122
Sawerthal, Henry 92,97
Scarlet Fever 28,29,75
Schomberg, Commodore C.M. 29, 130
Scully, Revd Patrick 13,14,20,49, 127
Simms, William 56,63,66
Simon's Town (Bay) 6,8,11,14,19, 29,32,47,57,64,86,103,115
Skirrow, John 16,17,18,19,23,25, 29,32,59,120
Skjellerup, J.F. 112
Smalley, George R. 60
Smiles, Samuel 84
Smith, Dr Andrew 6,28,70
Smyth, C. Piazzi 21,27,39,49,51,52, 55,56,57,58,60,61,62,63,80,85, 90,105,116,127,129
Smyth, Sir Henry A. 105
Smyth, Admiral W.H. 37,39,49
Somerset, Lord Charles 9,13,14, 23,28
South African College 60,62,69
South African Institution 28,69
South African Library 28,69,78,105, 106
South African Literary and Scientific Institution 69
South African Museum 6,32,56,69, 106
South African Philosophical Society 102,106,113
Spectroscopy 76,98,99,100,102,112
Spencer Jones, Sir Harold 114-117, 119,120,122,127
Stanley, H.M. 71
Steavenson, W.H. 121

Stone, Edward J. Chapter 4 passim, 84,85,86,98,112,127
Stoy, Richard H. 117,119-122,124, 127
Struve, F.G.W. 36,107
Sun, Eclipse of 4,76,114,118
Sutherland 123,124
Table Mountain 10,14,41,50,54,56, 57
Thompson, George 28,29
Thompson, J. Deas 31
Time Ball 47,49,63,64,65,74,80,86, 103,115
Time Gun 64,76,80,86,103
Time Signals 113,115
Transit Circle 63,66,69,73,75,86, 87,97,100,109,112,114,117,120
Transit Instrument 2,16,20,25,27, 28,32,50,51,65,69,92
Transit of Venus 82,83,89,90,98
Transit (Portable) 2,8,16,21,64,98
Troughton, Edward 2,6,13,56,66
Troughton and Simms, Messrs 66, 80,82,100
Tulbagh 18
Tygerberg 10
Union (Republic) Observatory 102
University of Cape Town 119,122
University of the Cape of Good Hope 78
Van Breda, Arend J. 9
Velocity of Sound 76
Warner, H.H. 97
Warren, Admiral Frederic 32,44,47
Watson, R. 115
Wauchope, Captain Robert 47
Wharton, Sir William 93,100,103, 106
Whittingdale, Col W. 105
Williams, Lieutenant John 52,57
Wind Tower 59,60,76,89,92,97,101, 115,117,122
Woods, C. Ray 92
Woolley, Sir Richard v.d.r. 122,125
Wynberg 11,44,45
Zenith Sector (Bradley's) 56,57